LOST ROADHOUSES OF SEATTLE

LOST ROADHOUSES OF SEATTLE

PETER BLECHA AND BRAD HOLDEN

THE
History
PRESS

Published by The History Press
Charleston, SC
www.historypress.com

Back cover: Generic highway motel matchbook cover. *Courtesy Northwest Music Archives.*

First published 2022

Manufactured in the United States

ISBN 9781467150736

Library of Congress Control Number: 2022936624

Highways and dance halls,
A good song takes you far,
You write about the moon,
You dream about the stars…

—*Danny O'Keefe, "The Road" (1972)*
Courtesy of Cotillion-Road Canon, BMI.

Highway roadhouses—where couples could dance and drink—made their major mark on the American scene between 1920 and 1950. Denounced from some pulpits as citadels of sin, they increased with the spread in ownership of the automobile. Along with the rest of the nation, that cluttered, neon-sign-lit stretch of pavement from Olympia to Everett had its share of dance pavilions beckoning revelers with entertainment.

—Seattle Times, *1975*

CONTENTS

Chapter 1

ROADSIDE ATTRACTIONS

Roadhouses were a fascinating American institution that have all but vanished from the old highways and remote roadways where they once flourished. A unique byproduct of early car culture, roadhouses initially offered lodging and a hot meal to weary travelers—although drinking and dancing were additional attractions provided at some. In the Seattle area, roadhouses appeared in several different variants: taverns, inns, rural "resorts," chicken dinner joints, halfway homes, supper clubs and dine-and-dance halls. While some of these establishments were little more than crudely constructed shacks, others were impressive structures that boasted formal ballrooms and ornate décor amid a cabaret-like atmosphere.

One commonality was that many openly flaunted liquor laws, and some allowed illegal gambling and prostitution, making them the frequent recipients of late-night police raids. Federal Prohibition agents—with badges out and guns in hand—were also regular

"Bootlegger's Song" song sheet (Seattle: Blue West Music Publishers, 1932). *Courtesy Northwest Music Archives.*

visitors, and one young Snohomish County district attorney, who would later become a U.S. senator, rose to political fame as a result of his zealous crackdown on local roadhouses. Providing ample fodder for titillating newspaper headlines, roadhouses represented the sordid underbelly of Seattle's peripheral nightlife.

In order to fully appreciate the saga of these decadent outposts, it is important to understand their historical backstory, and the logical starting point here really begins with the rise of car culture. The automobile was first invented in Europe, with numerous American companies soon following. It was in July 1900 that the first car ever seen driving along the streets of Seattle and Tacoma—a Chicago-made Woods Motor Vehicle Company electric unit—instantly captured the imagination of locals. Seattle historian Knute Berger once noted that "Ralph Hopkins, the proud possessor, was the lion of the hour. How popular he was with the girls; and how elated when a girl would exclaim that she had had an automobile ride." The popularity of autos understandably increased to such a level that the Washington State Highway Department was established in 1905; then, with the enactment of the State Aid Law in 1907, funds were made available for the construction and maintenance of new roads.

Meanwhile, though, Detroit's famed industrialist Henry Ford emerged, and his Ford Motor Company quickly grew to dominate the automotive market with its innovative manufacturing techniques. Ford's Model A debuted in 1903 but was then surpassed in 1908 by the Model T, which proved to be both simple to drive and easy to repair, making it by far the most popular car of its time. Ford's mass-production techniques were quickly adopted by other American manufacturers, and by the 1920s, Ford, General Motors and Chrysler had emerged as the "Big Three" auto companies. As a result, Americans began choosing cars as their primary means of transportation, which, in turn, would dramatically shape everyday life in the early twentieth century. Urban dwellers now had the opportunity to discover the beauty of the countryside, just as small-town residents grew to enjoy making shopping trips to the city. New roads, streets and early highways were quickly constructed to accommodate these new travelers, which in turn triggered an explosion of new roadside businesses. These included gas stations and restaurants with eye-grabbing architecture, as well as novelty roadside attractions that were specifically designed to capture the attention of passing motorists.

The popularity of automobiles also altered the scope of nightlife activities. Nocturnal revelers were no longer constrained to their neighborhood saloon, as newly constructed roadways now allowed motorists the opportunity to explore more remote destinations that could be enjoyed away from the prying eyes of local law enforcement. The earliest of these highway parlors were part of what was colloquially known as the "kerosene circuit"—public rooms lit by lanterns. These dimly lit and primitive venues were often tucked into wooded groves along muddy roads and provided the opportunity for people to gather together, enjoy copious amounts of some homemade hooch and dance to live music.

From these early roadside shanties emerged the area's earliest known roadhouses, which sprang up just outside the northern city limits—a choice made in an effort to evade scrutiny by the local police. This was a concept succinctly summarized in the slogan adopted by one rowdy joint located on the outer edge of Seattle proper: "Our Entertainment Begins Where the City's Limits End." These trailblazing outliers were situated along a windy and perilous stretch of road known as Golf Club Road. Today that street still exists in a tamer configuration known as Greenwood Avenue.

The two most notorious joints on Golf Club Road were the Greenlight and the North Seattle Automobile Club, which everyone simply referred to as "Duffy's Roadhouse." The tavern's namesake was its proprietor, Edward J. Duffy, who also owned and operated a number of saloons throughout Seattle. Duffy's Roadhouse operated from 1910 through 1912 and was also known as the Stone Castle, apparently due to its unique architecture. When Seattle booze parlors would close down for the night, people would pile into their jalopies, and "On to Duffy's!" became a popular late-night rallying cry. Quite often, these nocturnal merrymakers were of high school and college age, leading to some rather sordid rumors. In 1911, the *Seattle Times* sent one of its reporters to visit an unspecified Golf Club Road roadhouse in order to investigate the growing notoriety of these nightspots. The resulting article painted quite the unsavory picture:

> *All the accouterments of the standard roadhouse are there....There is the piano, the phonograph near it in the corner, the tables scattered around the room over which parties may drink their own liquor, and a none too particular register at the entrance of the establishment....The horrible fact remains that the roadhouse proposition, in all its ugliness and peril to young girls, apparently has become a fixture in that vicinity.*

Adding to all the negative publicity was the high number of car-related fatalities. The trek to these destinations was a perilous one, as Golf Club Road was dark and winding, and the drivers were often quite inebriated. As

This page: Duffy's Roadhouse (a.k.a. the Stone Castle), circa 1911. *Courtesy Shoreline Historical Museum.*

a result, there were several infamous car crashes along this route, eventually leading to the permanent closure of these early clubs. Despite their relatively short tenure, they would serve as the prototypes for the Prohibition-era roadhouses that would later arise north and south of the city.

Washington State was simultaneously in the midst of a contentious moral battle between the "wets" and the "drys"—supporters and opponents of legal liquor. At the heart of this battle was the proliferation of saloons, which had increasingly started dotting the rural landscape, as well as the astonishing level of turpitude and depravity that had overtaken Seattle. Major events, like the Yukon Gold Rush of 1896, had attracted thousands of people to the city, and local vice syndicates were happy to help satisfy their needs. Before long, saloons, cigar stores, gambling parlors, dance halls and brothels popped up, most of them located south of Yesler Way in an area that became known as the "Tenderloin District." At any given time, the streets would be crowded with men looking for a good time. Bordello owners would parade their girls up and down the streets on ornately decorated carriages, and barkers would stand outside the doors of saloons, loudly trying to entice new customers into their dens of iniquity amid the excited clatter of nearby gambling halls, billiard parlors and all-too-frequent street fights. As one local newspaper reported, "This part of town with its prostitution, dance and gambling halls, and cheap liquor bars and hotels are the abode of a great majority of the unmarried men who are constantly flowing in and out of the cities of the northwest."

For many local religious groups, things had grown so bad that immediate action needed to be taken. In the Midwest, groups such as the Woman's Christian Temperance Union (WCTU), the Anti-Saloon League and the Prohibition Party had grown into a powerful political voice whose sole intent was shutting down these troublesome establishments and bringing temperance to the masses. This anti-saloon sentiment soon spread throughout Washington, representing a larger and broader attitude that would soon engulf both local and national elections.

In Seattle, this newly formed temperance movement was led by Mark A. Matthews, a fire-and-brimstone Presbyterian minister. Known as "the black-maned lion" due to his long, thick head of hair, the tall and lanky Matthews let it be known that he was on a mission to rid Seattle of its sin and vice. He would often station himself outside the more popular saloons and give impassioned sermons, warning others about the moral dangers within such places. In one of his more famous tirades, he proclaimed, "The saloon is the most fiendish, corrupt, hell-soaked institution that ever crawled out of the slime of the eternal pit.…It takes your sweet innocent daughter, robs her of her virtue, and transforms her into a brazen, wanton harlot.…It is the open sore of the land!"

The WCTU and the Anti-Saloon League soon set up offices in downtown Seattle and joined Matthews on his quest to shut down these troublesome establishments. Together, this local temperance movement gathered enough signatures to put Washington Initiative Measure 3 on the state ballot. If successful with state voters, the 1914 initiative would prohibit the manufacture and sale of alcohol statewide. On November 3, state voters turned out in record numbers to decide on this important issue. After all the votes were tallied, Initiative Measure 3 officially became law with 189,840 voters in favor of the measure and 171,208 voters against it. Thanks to the organizational achievements of local temperance groups, Washington had now joined twenty-three other states in voting to go dry.

When this new law went into effect on January 1, 1916, state residents could still consume alcohol, but a legal permit was required to import it from out-of-state vendors. Quantity was limited to either a half gallon of hard liquor or a case (twenty-four bottles) of beer per month. Alcohol could also be obtained with a valid medical prescription, prompting the opening of hundreds of new pharmacies. Eventually, the right to buy out-of-state alcohol was removed as a legal privilege, thus establishing Washington as a truly dry state. A black market quickly opened up, paving the way for the first wave of regional bootleggers.

In Seattle, two rival gangs controlled black-market alcohol. One of these crews was headed by Edward Jack Margett (sometimes spelled Marquett), a former Seattle patrolman who was otherwise known as "Pirate Jack" due to his penchant for hijacking liquor shipments and selling the stolen alcohol from his Seattle headquarters. Battling Margett for control of the local booze market was a squad of bootleggers headed by a pair of brothers, Logan and Fred Billingsley. The conflict between the two groups often resulted in public shoot-outs, and the resulting violence eventually led to both groups being arrested and sent to prison.

That same year, various temperance groups galvanized their efforts into a nationwide grassroots movement that soon grew into a very powerful political coalition. With the anti-alcohol sentiment of the country growing at large, Congress passed the Eighteenth Amendment on January 16, 1919. The amendment prohibited the manufacture, sale, transportation and possession of alcohol. Ratified by the required two-thirds majority of the states in 1919, it effectively became the law of the land. A short time later, the Volstead Act (otherwise known as the National Prohibition Act) was enacted, which established the legal means for the federal government to enforce the Eighteenth Amendment. This new federal law was a lot stricter than Washington state prohibition had ever been and officially went into effect on January 17, 1920.

With federal Prohibition now in full swing, Seattle entered a new phase in this historic era. Taking advantage of the city's proximity to Canada, where booze was legal, a new wave of Seattle liquor rackets emerged to satisfy the growing demand for alcohol. Puget Sound rumrunners began using their high-powered speedboats—often powered by airplane engines purchased from nearby Boeing Airfield—to smuggle large quantities of Canadian booze into local ports. Once ashore, the crates of liquor would be loaded onto waiting trucks and cars and then distributed throughout the city by various liquor syndicates. The city's top scofflaw was a former Seattle police officer by the name of Roy Olmstead. Olmstead was known as "the King of the Puget Sound Bootleggers," and his operation kept the city awash in top-shelf Canadian spirits. In response, the Prohibition Bureau quickly set up an office in downtown Seattle in order to enforce the Volstead Act.

All along, speakeasies, gambling parlors and illegal inns had been openly operating within the Seattle city limits, and King County sheriff Claude G. Bannick had decided to make the closure of these establishments one of his top priorities. He frequently worked with federal agents from the Prohibition Bureau and mounted an aggressive campaign against any business engaged in the illegal sale of booze. He also went after dirty cops who were on the take from local bootleggers.

Seattle's most fabled speakeasy operator was one John Henry Hamilton (1891–1942). "Doc" Hamilton, as he was commonly known, had moved to Seattle in 1914 from West Point, Mississippi. During World War I, he served as a U.S. Army cook with the Ninety-Second Infantry, an African American contingent that was more commonly referred to as the "Buffalo Division." Then, upon the onset of Prohibition, Hamilton ran a speakeasy from his own apartment (at 107½ East Union Street), which was eventually raided by lawmen and shut down. Undeterred, he later opened his own successful restaurant/nightclub in the Central District neighborhood, and thus began a long, close association with his supplier, Roy Olmstead, and years and years of run-ins with the law. (More about all that in the chapters ahead.)

In response to Sheriff Bannick's crackdown, the proprietors of some Seattle roadhouses simply migrated north of the county line and set up shop along either of two new stretches of rural highway. The important thing is that they were now outside the jurisdiction of the Seattle police and the King County sheriff's department. This marks the period when these roadhouses exploded in popularity and quickly began proliferating north of the city.

Despite the efforts of law enforcement, such roadhouses remained popular throughout the duration of Prohibition and well beyond. However, the operation of these venues would change after the nation's booze laws were dismantled in 1933. One of the common misconceptions about Prohibition is that booze flowed freely again as soon as the Eighteenth Amendment was repealed and Americans went right back to drinking again, just as they had prior to 1920. This may have been true in some states, but it was certainly not the case in Washington. In fact, a new era of Prohibition emerged that became an important chapter in the saga of these local roadhouses. It began with the formation of the Washington State Liquor Control Board (WSLCB).

When the Eighteenth Amendment was repealed on December 5, 1933, and alcohol was made legal again, Washington State legislators were caught somewhat unprepared and, fearing a return to the lawless days of the saloons, quickly set up a special session to address these concerns. The Steele Liquor Act was passed on January 23, 1934, which established the WSLCB. The mission statement of this newly formed agency was to "protect the welfare, health, peace, morals, and safety of the people of the state." The board— which saw its mission as promoting "true temperance"—went out of its way to ensure that Washington State would avoid "the evils connected with the liquor traffic" and would never return to the lawless days of the saloons. As a result, the Steele Act outlined a series of strict rules intended to make sure that any new drinking establishments didn't become public menaces the same way that saloons had. Number one: drinking establishments could not serve any hard liquor, nor could beer and wine that was higher than 3.2 percent alcohol be sold.

Other rules reflected the general concerns people had about avoiding the lawlessness—including prostitution—of prior times. Therefore, women were no longer allowed to stand at the bar, nor could they order drinks for themselves. In addition, they had to be seated at all times so there could be no possibility of solicitation. This particular rule would stay in effect until 1969. The WSLCB also implemented a series of rules to avoid the bawdy reputations associated with prior saloon culture, including a rule that no vulgar or profane language could be used while inside a tavern. Additionally, there could be nothing "indecent" on the walls, and the interior of a tavern had to be visible from the street in order to minimize the risk of any illicit behaviors. To further keep things tame and in proper order, drink specials, happy hours and free food were not permitted, and closing time could be no later than one o'clock in the morning. Customers were required to be seated while drinking, as walking around or standing with a drink in your hand was now against the law. When it came to advertising, the board encouraged "conservative and dignified advertising," and newspaper ads were forbidden to show anyone actually consuming alcohol.

These new sets of rules joined earlier liquor laws that forbade the sale of liquor on Sundays, and together, they colloquially became known as "blue laws." Exempt from such rules were various private "social" or "educational" clubs—a suspiciously convenient legalistic wrinkle that allowed mainstream, and mainly white, organizations like the Eagles, Elks and Moose lodges to freely get their party on. In addition, there were still (until 1966) no liquor sales allowed on Sundays—well, except at the numerous local officers and enlisted men's clubs on local army, navy and air force bases.

Thanks to the Steele Act, these new liquor regulations carried the same weight as the law and were zealously enforced by a team of WSLCB agents. However, they did not deter the efforts of local roadhouses, whose mission had always been centered on evading local law enforcement in order to provide their customers a good time. In fact, many of these establishments were more than prepared for this new era of the WSLCB. For instance, when it came to the matter of hard liquor, many roadhouses creatively sidestepped the new law by allowing guests to smuggle in their own bottles of liquor, at which point they became known as "bottle clubs."

Customers looking to enjoy a fun evening of dancing, dining and drinking would typically arrive with their own bottle of booze (which was expected to be discreetly kept in a bag on the floor under each patron's table), and the house, in turn, offered a setup. Setups were usually included with the cover charge and included a bowl of ice, a pair of glasses and a quart of whatever mixer the person requested, such as ginger ale, sparkling soda water, fruit juices and so on. It was a clever way to bypass the new Steele Act. As for the new rules that forbade people from walking around with their drinks or required women to be dutifully seated, well—many roadhouse operators were too busy running gambling machines to be bothered enforcing such things.

In response, the WSLCB employed a small army of one hundred agents to enforce its rules and frequently raided any club suspected of allowing customers to bring their own booze inside or otherwise violating these new laws. This led to a new phase of Prohibition in which speakeasies were replaced with bottle clubs, the Volstead Act was superseded by the Steele Act and WSLCB deputies, instead of federal agents, were now the ones slapping handcuffs on people and hauling them off to jail.

With all this historical background out of the way, the roadhouses presented in this book cover both the speakeasy versions that were popular during Prohibition and the "bottle clubs" that remained popular throughout the 1930s and '40s. They were the physical embodiments of early car culture combined with the quest for fun during a time when liquor was being tightly controlled. By the end of World War II, many local roadhouses had been shuttered by the police due to alcohol and gambling violations. Those that remained shifted their focus over to music and dancing, effectively becoming nightclubs that were popular venues for Seattleites throughout the 1950s. Interestingly, this bottle club business model was the legally prescribed way of running a club right up until 1961, when political leaders—in anticipation of the throngs of visitors expected to attend the upcoming 1962 World's Fair—loosened a number of overly restrictive old laws pertaining to nightlife, including strict noise ordinances and rules for liquor establishments.

As music and entertainment trends changed over time, though, roadhouses gradually disappeared from the scene. While there were several different varieties, these roadside inns shared many commonalities that placed them under the same umbrella of illicit entertainment. They were the forbidden destination of those seeking a good time, and many were operated by flashy impresarios who boasted lengthy criminal rap sheets. These clubs were highly popular dancing venues showcasing well-known musical talent, but rather mysteriously, many met their demise by burning down under suspicious circumstances. While "progress" and the passage of time have slowly erased most of these places from the local landscape, their scandalous sagas live on in the following pages.

Chapter 2

LITTLE OLD SEATTLE

The history of booze, vice, crime and corruption in Seattle began not too long after the town's very founding. It was settled by the Denny Party in 1951, and that group's log cabins were soon joined by those of various newcomers—along with the area's first two commercial business enterprises. March 1852 saw the arrival of David "Doc" Maynard, who quickly built a cabin and opened a general store. Then, in October, Henry Yesler arrived by canoe and proceeded to build a steam-powered sawmill and wharf along Elliott Bay at Front/Commercial Street (today's First Avenue)—and Mill Street (today's Yesler Way).

Before long, these founders of the small village—originally dubbed "Duwamps"—were mingling not only with the friendly local Duwamish and Suquamish Natives but also, eventually, with loggers, seamen, miners, Chinese immigrants and all sorts of rank strangers who began passing through. Maynard quickly befriended the local Duwamish tribe's Chief Sealth, then convinced his fellow townies to formally rename the hamlet Seattle in his honor. It was in December 1852 that the Oregon territorial legislature formed King County and the citizens elected their first sheriff. In January 1853, Seattle was established as the county seat.

Interestingly, King County originally included a sizeable portion of land across Puget Sound on the Olympic Peninsula, but a number of Prohibition activists there objected to the saloon scene in Seattle and began agitating for the saloons' closure. This irritated the powers that be in Seattle, and Doc Maynard orchestrated the rise of a peninsular independence movement, which led to the redrawing of county lines and the establishing of Kitsap County.

It was also in 1853 that the U.S. Congress carved out the Washington Territory from the larger Oregon Territory. On August 25 of that year, another pioneer settler who'd traveled out west via the Oregon Trail, Thomas Mercer, arrived, complete with his team of horses and the village's first wagon. A few local young men helped him carve out a wagon path to his new land claim, and Mercer began offering the community his teaming services, hauling their goods to and from Yesler's Wharf. In 1854, Mercer also succeeded Arthur Denny as the King County commissioner—one with a keen awareness about the importance of roads.

Meanwhile, Doc Maynard—unlike most of the original Denny Party men—was a hard-drinking fellow, one who was not unhappy when prospective saloonkeepers began buying real estate lots from him. The "Maynard Town" neighborhood (situated just south of what would later become known as "Pioneer Square") began earning a certain reputation as a rough-and-tumble area whose attractions would come to include scores of saloons, dance halls and houses of ill repute. More than a few of these were situated along the first wagon road leading into, and out of, the village of Seattle, Military Road, which began on Front Street at Yesler's Mill, following an ancient Native footpath, then proceeded onward to Fort Steilacoom, forty-five miles to the south, and was completed in 1860.

The first of those scandalous dens of iniquity was founded in 1861 by John W. Pinnell, a tough newcomer who had previously operated successful brothels along San Francisco's notorious red-light district, the "Barbary Coast." Upon arrival in Seattle—by now a village of six hundred inhabitants—he immediately began earning his reputation as a corrupting influence on civic politics. According to the *Seattle Daily Intelligencer*, Pinnell had "propositioned the city fathers, offering them a yearly fee of $1,200 for the privilege of opening the sawmill town's first bordello," right near the town's biggest employer, Yesler's Sawmill. This fee would both provide the city with reliable income and allow "him to conduct his business without any threat from local law enforcement"—that is, the sheriff.

Pinnell soon got busy constructing a large rectangular building from rough-cut boards milled by Yesler. It would be the home of the Illahee, Pinnell's saloon/dance hall located at Second Avenue and Washington Street. That odd name was a Chinook jargon trading term meaning something like *earth, land, home; the place where one resides*. The Illahee boasted an expansive bar, an open dance floor and a series of private rooms where much of the wildest action took place. When the saloon was ready for business, Pinnell imported a musical tavern trio from Frisco, and thus began Seattle's rowdy nightlife. Over the following years, much carousing, crime and noise defined the joint, and the *Seattle Daily Intelligencer* reported that some of the "original settlers considered fighting to close the Illahee, but Pinnell had enough pull with the politicians in charge and hush money to keep his business going strong."

Still, a goodly portion of the town's more upright citizens simply despised Pinnell and resented the very presence of the Illahee. So there was little surprise when the *Seattle Daily Intelligencer* also reported that on May 7, 1878, an arsonist had struck and that "citizens and firemen stood about watching the fire.…Not a pint of water was thrown upon the fire, nor any effort made to save any part or article."

But the Illahee would be far from the only shady enterprise active in the area. At the southwest corner of Front Street and South Jackson Street stood the Felkner House hotel, which was managed by an Irishwoman named Mary Ann Conklin, who morphed the hotel into a bordello and whose foul-mouthed nature earned her the nickname of "Madame Damnable." Then along came Madame Lou Graham, who arrived in 1888 and founded her own brothel (nearby at Third and Washington Streets)—a haunt that was reportedly "frequented by Seattle's most elite business leaders and visitors"— before dying of syphilis at age forty-two. Considering all this debauchery, the town's more refined families began referring to the whole area "below the line"—Mill Street—as the town's "tenderloin district" and the "Lava Bed."

Meanwhile, Henry Yesler's sawmill had maintained its role as Seattle's leading business. And because timber destined for the mill was physically skidded out of the forest and down muddy Mill Street, that route soon earned the sobriquet of "Skid Road." It was a phrase that soon came to be associated with the dubious denizens thereof, whose lives were said to be "on the skids." Such monikers decidedly did not elevate the seedy neighborhood's sketchy reputation. Added to that, the blocks between Second and Third along Washington Street also became the heart of Seattle's early Chinatown, an area where gambling and opium use were rampant. Add to all that the founding of a rowdy gambling joint called the Union Club (at Second and Washington Street)—which was run by Wyatt Earp, the fabled gambler, gunslinger, brothel bouncer and onetime sheriff of Tombstone, Arizona, who'd gained notoriety via the legendary 1881 gunfight at the O.K. Corral incident—and the picture becomes clearer. This truly was the Wild West. With the constant arrival of ever more newcomers, as well as transients passing through, Seattle saw an expectable uptick in crime, and in the 1880s, the formation of an actual police department was finally deemed necessary.

Still, the community's more genteel members gamely tried to place a more palatable name on the area. And because the village's first Catholic church (located directly across the street from Lou Graham's building) was commonly referred to as the "White Chapel," efforts were made to dub the whole neighborhood the "Whitechapel District." Nice try.

Adding to this whole chaotic milieu, several pioneering breweries were founded on land situated just south of town and along the bay and the Duwamish River. As an example of the poor reputation of the area, one can look back to the case of one of the Bayview Brewery's workers, a German immigrant named Henry Crämer. In August 1894, he was arrested, accused and tried—based entirely on circumstantial evidence—of robbing and murdering one Phillipina Müller and her child, even though his reputation within the German community was otherwise untarnished. Crämer's defense attorney, Otto Frederick Wegener, tried to focus the court's attention on the blatant corruption within local politics at the time and posited that the chief of police, Bolton Rogers, was simply using Crämer's case to deflect attention from his own past misdeeds by trying to wrap up the murder mystery without a fair investigation.

The sensational death penalty trial received nationwide publicity, and Wegener went on to publish a booklet in which he expounded on the dangers of that time and place: "Since the whole area of South Seattle is notoriously unsafe, the depository of numerous tramps and suspects, and is close to the water, where the criminals can easily escape by boat without a trace, the public demanded the discovery of the perpetrator of this most brutal double murder, and that he be brought to justice.…For years the ruling party in Seattle has made it a rule to elect a man as chief of police who has a political 'pull' in the city's Whitechapel district. This part of town with its prostitution, dance and gambling halls, and cheap liquor bars and hotels are the abode of a great majority of the unmarried men who are constantly flowing in and out of the cities of the northwest," and local elections "are controlled by the owners of the playhouses, who turn a blind-eye or both eyes from the frequent transgressions of these people," creating "a great nuisance through this political pull."

The years went by, and many changes occurred here—including the Great Seattle Fire of June 6, 1889, in which much of the town's central business district was burned to the ground—but some things never seem to change, and Seattle's original old town Skid Row neighborhood would long be known for its nightlife debauchery, crime and corrupt law enforcement.

In the decades before automobiles were a common sight on city streets and paved roads leading out of town didn't yet exist, urban fun-seekers found exciting action in a number of nightspots located within the city limits. Scattered from Belltown to Chinatown, from East Madison Street to South Jackson Street, convenient public restaurants, taverns and dance halls all dependably drew happy crowds. And so, too, did the untold numbers of "secret" speakeasies. Indeed, a local trumpeter named Billy Stewart would later recall that "on 1st Avenue in Belltown there was a speakeasy every other door. And about every other houseboat on Lake Union was a speakeasy, too. I know, because around 1930 I had a houseboat there myself." These joints were not difficult to find, and so they also inevitably attracted the unwanted attentions of the Seattle Police Department, Washington state liquor control agents and prosecutors and judges both local and federal.

The Rose Room

The most fabled of all Seattle-area venues that played central roles during the early Prohibition era's speakeasy craze was the Hotel Butler's Rose Room—which also happened to be based in the oldest building of them all. It was during those first smoky hours following the Great Seattle Fire that local businessman Guy C. Phinney bought a large, charred lot at the corner of Second Avenue and James Street—the former site of Hillory Butler's 1875 homestead—and quickly began construction of the five-story Butler Block office building. In 1894, the building was converted into a hotel, which would instantly be acknowledged as Seattle's first "big city" hotel, complete with its own restaurant, the Butler Grill.

Opened in 1890, the Hotel Butler (at 114 James Street) would, in time, host bigwig visitors, including Presidents Teddy Roosevelt, Grover Cleveland and William McKinley; railroad magnate James J. Hill; Wild West showman Buffalo Bill; famed actress Lillian Russell; and the Alaskan gold rush crime boss Soapy Smith. In 1903, new owners added two floors, which included Seattle's fabulous new watering hole and ballroom, the Rose Room. Things went smoothly until Prohibition came along in 1916—but the Butler found ways to meet the challenge, an effort appreciated by their thirsty clientele. "Liquor, was not sold by the House," Seattle businessman Henry Broderick once wrote, "but in some devious, if not exactly mysterious way."

That beverage service was, as the *Seattle Times* would note, "surreptitious: The waiters served ice and ginger ale. Bellboys produced the bourbon, Scotch or gin—or good wines at about $1.50 a jug." This is where Seattle's infamous "tolerance policy" came into effect. Everyone knew what was going

Left: The Hotel Butler, undated postcard. *Courtesy Northwest Music Archives.*

Opposite: Vic Meyers's Hotel Butler Orchestra, circa 1920s. *Courtesy Northwest Music Archives.*

on in what had become Seattle's most prominent speakeasy—indeed, plenty of the town's social and political elites enjoyed sipping smuggled Canadian booze well into the wee small hours at the nightspot—and, according to the *Seattle Times*, "as long as they could, city officials in charge of the police looked the other way. Every now and then they would make a token raid on the Rose Room, netting bellboys and perhaps a waiter—under the old 'license by fine' system." After paying a small fine, those employees would be right back to work. And between these fines, the occasional bribe and, eventually, regular payoffs to the Seattle Police Department's "bag men"— an ongoing practice that wasn't fully exposed until the late 1960s—the fun times continued with generally minimal disruptions.

It was in 1919 that a young bandleader named Victor Meyers first brought his ten-man dance band to the Rose Room to play for trendy raccoon coat-

garbed college men and their bobbed-hair flapper dates, who danced the Black Bottom, Charleston and Collegiate Shag in a frenzy. In what became a point of humor, Meyers would regularly tip off all the attendees to an imminent liquor raid by signaling his combo to halt whatever song they were on and shift to the chorus of a popular song, "The Near Future." Penned by Irving Berlin, it was a comedic tune that made its debut in the *Ziegfeld Follies of 1919*. The song's chorus was the hook, one that is easily remembered to this day: "How dry I am, how dry I am, / It's plain to see, just why I am, / Oh, how I call for alcohol, / And that is why so dry I am." Well, *remembered*, that is, only in part and mainly because it was eventually bastardized into a little ditty mocking the "drys" with naughty new lyrics: "How dry I am, how wet I'll be, / If I don't find the bathroom key, / I found the key, now where's the door? / It's too late now, it's on the floor."

With that inspiring refrain in the air, the Rose Room staff knew to pour all the evidence down the kitchen drains, while the attendees abandoned their drinks. One widely publicized raid on November 13, 1927, resulted in the arrest of more than 150 merrymakers. "While the orchestra wailed 'How Dry I Am,' a score of uniformed policemen joined the police dry squad late Saturday, 'College Night,' in a raid....Hundreds of glasses were shattered

TO MEET A POPULAR
DEMAND

VIC
MEYERS

WILL RETURN
TO THE

HOTEL ·BUTLER
ROSE ROOM
SATURDAY

JUNE 24TH

For An Extended
Engagement.

He Will Personally
Conduct His New

14 PIECE BAND

The largest and finest
in the city.

DINNER AND
SUPPER

DANCING

Rose Room display ad promoting Vic Meyers' dance band. *The* Seattle Post-Intelligencer, *June 24, 1933.*

and the contents spilled when patrons became aware of the raid and dancers slopped their way through a small stream of liquid in their circuit of the dance floor….Arrests were made based on the finding of either bottles or glasses on or under tables."

That was a particularly infamous incident, but raids were hardly uncommon. As one local magazine reflected a few years later, "It was all in the course of an evening's fun to have the prohibition agents swoop in, seize partially concealed bottles of liquor from under the tables, perhaps arrest an employee or two, and then depart amid boos and not-too-subtle insults." Fun for revelers, perhaps, but the risk to owners and managers was that of legal abatement: a suit typically affecting the defendant's tax liability in a negative way that can cause a business to be forcibly shuttered.

So, indeed, not all such incidents had any humorous aspect to them. Just a few blocks away from the Rose Room had been a notorious crime nest, Luigi Romeo's London Pool Hall (at 507 King Street), where a police officer was killed during a raid. Then, mere months later, on September 30, 1926, federal agents stormed the hall and proceeded to demolish it with axes. Yet another big raid on the Rose Room by Prohibition agents occurred on December 20, 1928, followed by another on June 1. As the *Seattle Post-Intelligencer* put it, "The 'Rose Room,' they all agreed, was invariably heavy with scent—but of alcohol, not blossoms. One agent later testified during an abatement proceeding in court: 'So much liquor was being consumed, that I could smell it as soon as I entered the Rose Room. There were bottles of whisky and gin on top of tables and underneath—and no signs of any food being served." Another agent testified that while opening a bottle for him and his partner, a waiter told them, "Say, boys, there's a big crowd here tonight and you can't tell what'll happen. Put the bottle on the floor and kick it over if there's a raid."

Even though these periodic raids were played up in the local newspapers, it still took many years for the clampdown to have any real effect. Meanwhile, other history had been made here: in 1923, a field crew from Brunswick Records rolled into town and recorded a few songs with the Hotel Butler Orchestra in the Rose Room, which resulted in the release of "Shake It and Break It," the very first commercially marketed 78 rpm disc (Brunswick Records No. 2501) ever cut in Seattle. Later, in 1928, Meyers cowrote a new foxtrot tune, "Ada," that was named after a popular waitress there and that his band recorded for Columbia Records (No. 1530-D). Yet another disc featured them playing "Rose Room" (Columbia No. 2120-D). Meyers's band also began broadcasting live three days a week over at Roy and Elsie Olmstead's private home-based radio station, KFQX.

Vic Meyers's "Ada" song sheet (Seattle: West Coast Music Publishers, 1928). *Courtesy Northwest Music Archives.*

Then, after a decade-long run of illicit revelry, the Rose Room finally attracted the unwanted attentions of local temperance activists, including the Reverend Dr. Mark A. Matthews, who caused federal charges to be filed, and in May 1929 the place was punished via judicial decree. Although the Butler Grill and Rose Room did reopen for business, the bloom was off the rose, and its most exciting days were through. The hotel was shuttered during the Great Depression in 1933 and auctioned off in 1934, and a few years later, the top five stories were removed and the bottom two converted into a parking garage.

Doc Hamilton's Barbecue Pit

In August 1924, "Doc" Hamilton resurfaced, doubling down on his previous experience of running a speakeasy in his apartment by reentering the underworld nightlife biz. It was then that he incorporated a formal new enterprise: his namesake Doc Hamilton's Barbecue Pit, founded with a truly impressive $15,525 in capital stock—or nearly $250,000 in today's dollars. He built the nightspot in a storefront (at 908 Twelfth Avenue), and during the peak of Prohibition, the joint became one of the city's hottest and most brazen speakeasies—one that was even favored by many prominent businessmen, not to mention Seattle mayor Edwin J. Brown.

In his book about the history of jazz in Seattle, *Jackson Street After Hours*, Paul de Barros offers this description of the notorious nightspot:

> *Limousines lined the curb out front, while Seattle's social* [elite], *including the mayor, ducked in and out of the club....Downstairs was the "action"—roulette and an all-night dice game. Should there be a raid, the Barbecue Pit was prepared. A complete alarm system, with a complicated system of bells, bars, and pulleys, snaked through the building. A button convenient to...the cashier at the lunch counter was wired to a buzzer at the triple-barred doors of the cabaret basement.*

Often compared to Harlem's famous Cotton Club, the Pit was renowned for its elegantly decorated interior, delicious food, live jazz music and the presence of Hamilton, who was known for his warm hospitality and often described by local newspapers as "a genial host with a golden smile." At any given time, Hamilton could either be found tending to things in the kitchen or out on the floor, personally welcoming guests as they arrived and occasionally singing for his crowds.

But the main attraction was, of course, the Pit's large inventory of top-shelf booze, courtesy of Roy Olmstead's bootlegging operation. Olmstead, Seattle's top bootlegger at the time, supplied the Barbecue Pit with much of its top-shelf booze. As Hamilton's club increased in popularity, he quickly became one of the liquor kingpin's biggest customers, and the two men formed a close business relationship. As a result, when Olmstead was eventually arrested by federal Prohibition officials, Hamilton—and eighty-nine others—found themselves indicted as well.

The resulting trial, known as the "Whispering Wires Case," would prove to be one of the biggest liquor trials in the nation's history. The trial's jury selection process began on January 19, 1926, and the *Seattle Times* quoted one of Hamilton's friends trying to console him in the courtroom by saying, "If they ever convict these boys, they'll have to give them suspended sentences." Hamilton replied, "How's that?" "Well, the jails are all full now and they won't have any place to put them." Further newspaper accounts would note that the seemingly unworried Hamilton slept through most of the subsequent proceedings. At one point he complained to those sitting behind him, "If they don't get some action soon, I'll have to get some barbecue sandwiches from my place and pass them around." Two days later, he made good on his promise and provided a "heaping tray of sandwiches" for the entire courtroom that, according to one newspaper account, were swiftly consumed. In another instance, he perked up from his slumber when a clerk read a newspaper article out loud to the court that mentioned Hamilton's name, causing the club owner to stand up and flash a big smile that was said to be "infectious," causing others in the courtroom to also break out smiling.

The conspiracy trial ended on February 20, 1926, with the conviction of twenty-one defendants, including Roy Olmstead and his attorney, Jerry Finch. Rather surprisingly, Hamilton was found not guilty and acquitted of all charges. It's unknown if his delicious sandwiches or noteworthy smile had any influence over the verdict, but after his acquittal, Hamilton immediately returned to his duties at the Barbecue Pit, serving as Seattle's unofficial ambassador of vice. Gambling ran nearly around the clock at Hamilton's joint, with a very well-stocked bar, delicious food and music provided by some of the city's top jazz bands. Staying somewhat cautious, Hamilton installed an alarm system throughout the club that would alert everyone to an impending police raid, thereby giving his customers ample time to discard any drinks, hide any gambling devices and, hopefully, escape out into the back alley.

A year later, on April 3, 1927, Hamilton's security system was put to the test when a phalanx of Seattle police officers and federal Prohibition agents conducted a surprise raid on the Barbecue Pit. According to the *Seattle Times*, the raid was carried out "while merriment was at its height," and Hamilton was immediately placed under arrest and charged with an assortment of gambling and liquor violations. Fifteen guests were also arrested that night, some of whom were described as being "prominent in the city's business circles." Police reported that Hamilton's alarm buzzers had indeed worked as intended but had been drowned out by the loud music of the jazz band.

Despite all the incriminating evidence, Hamilton emphatically denied being knowledgeable of any

Doc Hamilton enjoying the good life, undated photo. *Courtesy Blackpast.org.*

Doc Hamilton's Barbecue Pit, Seattle, May 25, 1931. *Courtesy Northwest Music Archives.*

The Barbecue Pit's basement dance hall, May 25, 1931. *Courtesy Northwest Music Archives.*

Oscar William Holden at his piano, Seattle, 1920s. *Courtesy of Linda Holden Givens.*

illegal activity. Speaking to local reporters from the jail, he explained, "I haven't had anything to do with gambling or liquor. I just want my guests to enjoy themselves and if some dice fell out of someone's pocket and a little innocent game started, I was too busy roasting chicken to notice." He added, "No sir, not me....I put signs up on the wall that gambling was not allowed.... Somebody sure must have brought those dice with them."

During his trial in May, Hamilton tried to plea bargain with the judge by explaining that he had just purchased a dog that had been specially trained to bark if it heard the click of dice. Beaming his trademark grin, Doc assured the judge that he would keep the dog on the premises at all times, thereby putting an immediate stop to any surreptitious gambling activity. Unfortunately for Hamilton, the dog story didn't grant him any clemency, and the less-than-amused judge sentenced Hamilton to sixty days in jail. That experience is likely what prompted Hamilton, upon release, to consider opening a new business—actually, two of them—beyond the city limits and north of the county line, away from the scrutiny of Seattle law enforcement. (More about all that in chapters 4 and 6.)

Chapter 3

THE THREE OLD ROADS

I t was in the summer of 1858 that the U.S. Army began surveying a new wagon route between Fort Steilacoom, located just south of Tacoma, up through Seattle and onward to Fort Bellingham. The planked road was to be built in two segments that would meet at Seattle, but by October 1860 only the first—the southern—portion of the Military Road had been completed. The portion heading straight northward from Seattle—basically from Yesler's Wharf, up and behind Denny Hill (near today's Belltown neighborhood), then along the eastern edge of today's Queen Anne Hill and beyond toward Bellingham—remained not much more than a rough trail for a good while still. In time, it was developed as the North Trunk Road, which later evolved into the "Seattle-Everett Highway," where plenty of wild roadhouse action would occur. (More about all that in chapter 6.)

Meanwhile, up into the 1880s, folks seeking to head north from Seattle by land necessarily had to navigate the third road, a more easterly route that became known as the "old Bothell Road," which led them up and over to Everett. As it happened, the majority of local roadhouses would be situated along those two different northbound routes, and as such, they were the scene of much revelry, drinking and dancing—not to mention countless law enforcement efforts. One thing that all these halls had in common was their strategically selected locations: perched just beyond the posted "City Limits" signs.

The Bothell Road

It was in 1884 that a Norwegian immigrant, Gerhard Ericksen, arrived in Seattle; in 1886, he staked a claim at the north end of Lake Washington. Ericksen and his wife, Dorothea, then built a home and general store (at today's Northeast 183rd Street and Bothell Way), and he soon became the local postmaster. But in the wake of the 1893 depression, he gave up the store and got involved in the lumber industry. The challenge he faced, though, was that of transporting lumber down to Seattle. What was needed was a direct road, and he helped prod the Washington State legislature to pass the 1903 Good Roads Act. From there, Erickson got himself elected to the legislature. In 1905, he sponsored a bill that created the Washington State Highway Department and also authorized the construction of a dozen new roads.

One of those was to be named—albeit misspelled!—the Gerhard Erickson Road, a muddy wagon route that led from David Bothell's namesake townsite down to Seattle's Tenth Avenue Northeast (today's Roosevelt Way Northeast) and onward to downtown. Goodly portions of it eventually would be reconfigured a bit as the Bothell Road, which was later designated as a branch of the Pacific Highway.

In January 1914, an event was promoted to celebrate the road's completion, and Erickson delivered a dedication speech, which included these lines: "It is with the greatest of pleasure that I see so many distinguished citizens here to help celebrate the greatest event in the history of our town, that is the opening of the Pacific Highway from Seattle to Bothell. Thirty years ago, I found my way through the dense forest and took up my homestead one mile north of here. At that time there was no town known as Bothell on the map—just the wild woods. The nearest place to buy provisions was Seattle, and a good many hardships were encountered by us when it came to getting the necessary provisions up for the log cabin on our homestead....Hard work by many of our pioneers with the help of some of your progressive citizens in Seattle finally persuaded the County Commissioners to listen to our petitions for a better road. The results are what you have seen today when you came up in your automobiles from Seattle to Bothell, which formerly took the better part of a day. Thirty years we have talked over it, dreamed about it and now we are proud over it. We want you all to see it and enjoy riding over one of the best roadways that was ever built by men."

In 1918, considerable efforts were made to improve the road, which, according to the *Seattle Times*, originally had "fourteen sharp curves and four bridges," while the new version had only "four curves of wide radius and no bridges." Now, it was considered an "arterial highway," and it was a major route leading northward from the city center—via Stewart Street, to Eastlake Avenue, to Tenth Avenue Northeast, to Bothell—and over to Everett (a portion of which was upgraded as State Route 527 in 1969).

Meanwhile, the private ownership of motorized vehicles was increasing at a phenomenal rate, and that fueled the construction of ever more roadways. Just consider that back in 1903, Detroit's Ford Motor Company sold a total of 1,708 of its Model A cars. But by 1913, that annual sales figure had skyrocketed to 168,220 Model T cars sold. By 1923, the roads across America were being utilized by 1,831,128 new Fords—not to mention the 300,000 Chevys, 200,000 Buicks, 150,000 Dodges and 146,000 Studebakers that joined them. And all this was still a good three decades prior to the dawn of America's interstate freeway system in the 1950s.

The government responded to this increasing need for new and upgraded roads. It was prodded along by various new organizations, including the Automobile Club of Western Washington. The need was obvious. The year 1900 saw the very first automobile arrive in Seattle. By 1906, the whole of Washington State could boast a total of about seven hundred motor vehicles; by 1916, that figure had grown to nearly seventy thousand.

Therefore, by early 1920, King County had prepared an aggressive program to add "many miles of new and scenic" routes of paved highways that they promised would "be available for motor traffic this summer," according to the *Seattle Times*. Among the roads selected for upgrades was the old Bothell Road, which that same year was rerouted, paved and—in a burst of postwar pride—renamed "Victory Way" to honor the service of those Americans who served during World War I (1917–18). The road was completed in 1922 and promoted as the "New State Highway." Victory Way as a name—despite all the pomp and good intentions (complete with the erection of a "Welcome Arch" over the roadway at Northeast Eighty-Ninth Street)—never truly took hold among the public, and it was more commonly referred to as the "Bothell Highway" (today's Bothell Way, with its more southerly strip renamed Lake City Way and the whole thing eventually dubbed State Route 522).

The phenomenal increase in the availability of automobiles was literally changing people's eating habits, and as *Seattle Times* columnist John J. Reddin once noted, "roadside restaurants and roadhouses were springing up like mushrooms, especially on the Bothell and Everett Highways." The roadhouses deliberately ran afoul of the law, though, and so they were the recipients of frequent police raids and the subjects of countless newspaper headlines. The more westward route—the Seattle-Everett Highway (with the northern section still extant as today's Aurora Avenue North)—mostly eschewed chicken dinners in favor of gambling and prostitution, thus attracting a much rowdier customer base. The clubs located along the second route, the Bothell Road, had a wide assortment of roadhouses that were very akin to the honky-tonks and juke joints of the American South. They were where locals went to enjoy a nice chicken dinner, dance to some live music and imbibe some illicit hooch.

SOUTH X NORTHEAST

Numerous roadhouses built along the Bothell Highway in the early twentieth century would, as it happened, feature southern culture themes and down-home cuisine offerings, especially fried chicken dinners. This likely occurred because astute businessmen recognized the arrival here of an increasing number of immigrants from the Deep South who were understandably a bit homesick. Or maybe it was just because that "comfort food" was tasty. Either way, as Catherine Roth once wrote, "southern and minstrel-themed fried chicken restaurants were attracting Seattleites who, according to Hattie Graham Horrocks' vintage guide to Seattle restaurants, 'wished to drive out-of-town for the occasional dinner.'"

BRIARCREST RANCH

The first roadside destination dining venue to open along the old Bothell Road was at Jack Babb and his wife's rural farm, located up at 155th Street

Briar Crest Lodge display ad. *The Seattle Times, June 25, 1928.*

and the Bothell Road, which was originally called Babb's Ranch. It opened for business in 1913, and its name was later upgraded to the Briarcrest Ranch. The couple pioneered the southern-theme marketing concept by offering "for your Sunday dinner, fried spring chicken, Southern style." By 1915, dancing opportunities had been added. The Babbs were well aware of the alterations underway within society—the "increasing availability of automobiles [was changing] the course and focus of entertainment establishments. New roads beckoned drivers, and soon those businesses with an entrepreneurial spirit were finding ways to lure travelers beyond the sphere of Seattle's downtown dance halls," according to the Shoreline Historical Museum.

In time, Babb would place inviting advertisements stating: "When motoring north of Seattle go to Briarcrest Ranch"; the ads touted Briarcrest's "pleasant parlors for dancing" and "famous Fried Chicken Dinner from $1.50 to $1.00. Greatest dinner ever served anywhere for the price." In 1928, Mrs. Thomas J. Cassutt and Mrs. Louise R. Shinn bought the place and ran it as the Briar Crest Lodge, where they offered chicken dinners, "Dinner Dances," and "Frat and Sorority Functions."

My Southern Home and Mammy's Shack

In 1919, Briarcrest Ranch was joined by My Southern Home, which became a destination joint renowned for its practice of "frying chicken in the window in plain sight of passersby." In 1921, it was followed by Bob's Place, which was "Famous for Butterkist Fried Chicken" ("worth crowing about") and its outdoor booths—so "famous," or at least popular, that the establishment survived into the 1970s. Then in 1923 came Otto and Pearl Hammergren's Mammy's Shack, credited with being "the originators of the chicken-on-toast idea all cooked by a real southern mammy." It became an overnight sensation, inspiring caravans of motorists to venture out from the brick-paved streets in town and hack their way northward from Seattle out to the forested boondocks to check it out. By 1925, J.C. Jackson was operating his Highway Sandwich Shop out of his automobile service station. And in the wake of all this success, scores of other entrepreneurs opened their own roadside eateries and "resorts," and it became a popular social thing for city folk to hop into their cars for weekend excursions along the Bothell Highway.

Uncle Tom's Cabin and the Dixie Inn

Over time, a local tradition evolved around the annual seasonal grand opening of the dining and dancing "resorts" located all up and down the Bothell Highway. The *Seattle Times* celebrated one year by noting that the "Pleasure Resorts Prepare for Summer Traffic; Roomy Dance Pavilions....

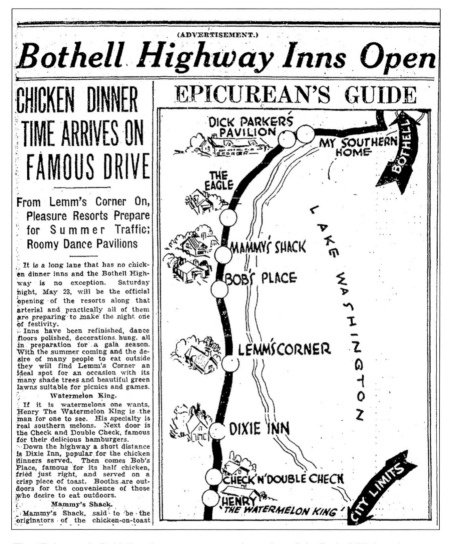

The "Epicurean's Guide" to the summer seasonal opening of the Bothell Highway's roadside attractions. *The* Seattle Times, *May 22, 1931.*

Saturday night, May 23, will be the official opening of the resorts along that arterial and practically all of them are preparing to make the night one of festivity. Inns have been refinished, dance floors polished, decorations hung, all in preparations for a gala season."

An "Epicurean's Guide" map published in the *Seattle Times* highlighted some of the attractions. Among them was Henry J. "the Watermelon King" Lemm's fruit stand, whose slogan was "Real Southern WATERMELONS Our

Left: Mammy's Shack matchbook, undated. *Courtesy Northwest Music Archives.*

Right: Uncle Tom's Cabin matchbook, undated. *Courtesy Northwest Music Archives.*

Specialty." Evidently this was still a time when potential customers might drive all the way across town to access such imported "ice cold" produce. Lemm also ran a nearby resort, Lemm's Corner, which featured "cabins with or without bedding—picnic grounds and games free. The only green spot on the highway," along with one-dollar chicken dinners.

Left: Dixie Inn display ad promoting dining and "Dancing Every Night." *The* Seattle Times, *1931.*

Right: Uncle Tom's Cabin matchbook interior graphic, undated. *Courtesy Northwest Music Archives.*

Then many more opportunistic joints popped up, such as Joe's Hot Lunches (at 125th East and Bothell Way)—which, curiously enough, didn't even sport a lunch counter. Instead, Joe sold barbecued meats "to go" along with jugs of bootleg booze he hid in various hollowed-out tree stumps around his property.

Other nearby joints included Tom Meeker's regrettably conceived Uncle Tom's Cabin (located nearby at Northeast 115th Street and 15th Avenue Northeast) and the Dixie Inn, which featured "Dancing Every Night" (on their thirty-eight-by-forty-foot dance floor) to the Dixie Inn Orchestra and was "popular for the chicken dinners served," not to mention their special "Whoopie Nite every Wednesday." Meanwhile, the Eagle Inn was "featuring chicken and steak dinners." There was also Coe's Country Club (at 10830 Roosevelt Way), which opened in 1938 and offered southern fare, including pan-fried chicken with hot biscuits and honey, and dancing to country music by the Hayloft Hillbillies as well as local stars like "Texas Jim" Lewis, "Bashful Billy" Lee, Paul Tutmarc and Jack Rivers. Then there was the Porterhouse and, finally, located between Mammy's Shack and the Dixie Inn, yet another "chicken dinner resort"/hotel called the Mexicano.

Hittin' the Road

Roadside resorts often grew into highly successful, and lucrative, businesses—at least in part because area taxicab companies had established favorable rates to ferry carless people from in-town locations way out to the far reaches of the Bothell Highway. Those taxi customers included roadhouse patrons as well as employees—cooks and waiters—of the various establishments.

As far back as 1919, King County engineers counted as many as ten thousand cars a day using the road, and within a few years, traffic jams were becoming a common occurrence. Traffic along the route rapidly ticked up after May 1920, when a whole new 220-acre planned residential neighborhood called Victory Heights (at Northeast Ninety-Fifth Street) began selling its 425 lots and construction of the first homes began.

As traffic increased, a new phenomenon arose: the sudden emergence of traffic jams. By July 1924, traffic bottlenecks—and terrible car wrecks—were regularly in the local news. On July 28, 1924, the *Seattle Post-Intelligencer* reported that "motor traffic on Victory Way between Bothell and Seattle became so congested yesterday afternoon that state highway police were unable to cope with the situation unaided....[They] telephoned William Barr, assistant county jail superintendent for sheriff's deputies to assist them."

It comes as no surprise that wrecks along streets and highways were increasingly frequent occurrences as greater numbers of neophyte drivers acquired automobiles—and local newspapers never missed an opportunity to milk these situations with overblown headlines. For example, in November 1924, the *Seattle Times* covered an incident near one eatery with this blaring headline: "Three Men Escape Death in Accident on Highway." The article itself calmly explained that the men "narrowly missed being seriously injured when their automobile ran into an embankment on the roadway's perilous curve near Mammy's Shack on the Bothell Highway last night." A few years later, another headline—"Three Escape Death as Car Overturns"—relayed how a veteran Seattle police officer and his wife and child were in a "freak accident on the Bothell Highway near Mammy's Shack." Officer Herbert had the misfortune of clipping a stalled car and flipping his car onto its roof in a roadside ditch.

In short, the roadway was winding and dangerous—at one point it was deemed "the worst highway in the state"—and the traffic pulling in and out of the area's many resorts increased the risks for everyone, including one of the owners of Mammy's Shack, Pearl Hammergren, who was jailed on drunk driving charges one night after crashing her car into another driver while heading southward on the wrong side of the road.

THE "BOTTLE HIGHWAY"

The Roaring Twenties was a period of fast-paced change. That decade not only saw the emergence of the radio broadcasting and record production industries, but it also became known as the Jazz Era. This new music brought out hordes of young bearskin coat–clad dandies and their feather-boa-and-spangle-bedecked coed flapper dates, who did all the crazy new fad dances like the foxtrot, Lindy Hop, shimmy, Sugar Foot Strut and Varsity Drag. Young folks especially loved to cruise around the area in their jalopies, seeking fun of both the legal and illicit varieties.

But those who didn't want to risk going into the frequently raided speakeasies downtown—or any of the back-alley joints in Chinatown— were understandably attracted to venues located in areas outside the legal jurisdiction of the Seattle police. Luckily for them, a string of fabled

Left: Coe's Country Club display ad. *The* Seattle Times, *May 19, 1939.*

Right: The Red Top Cab Company's display ad promoting their service outside the Seattle city limits. *The* Seattle Times, *January 26, 1924.*

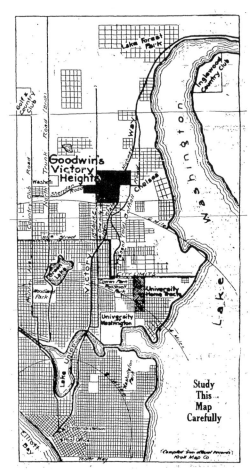

Left: Map showing staggered 1920 city limits lines at Northeast Sixty-Second and Northeast Eighty-Fifth Streets and the site of the new Victory Heights neighborhood. *The* Seattle Post-Intelligencer, *May 2, 1920.*

Below: Plantation display ad promoting chicken and steak dinners, plus "Dancing Every Evening." *The* Seattle Times, *November 25, 1925.*

The Plantation

roadhouses arose just outside of Seattle's official city limits. Located along winding unlit roads out in the sticks, such nightspots could lay low enough to stay relatively safe from the prying eyes of the King County sheriff and his posse. One such route was a good six-mile-long section of the Bothell Highway—just north of the city limits at Northeast Eighty-Fifth Street—which came to develop a reputation for its string of dining and dancing "resorts" that featured restaurants, dance halls, rentable cabins and, in many cases, illicit liquor. There were so many resorts, in fact, that King County sheriff Claude E. Bannick cleverly disparaged the Bothell Highway as the "Bottle Highway." He also took to describing the roadhouses as "drinking resorts."

Some of these roadhouses had simple monikers—like the Blue Bird, Bungalow Inn, Canyon Park Inn, the Lake View, Mae's Place, Otto's Place, the Plantation, the Toot Inn and the Tip-Top Inn ("Dinner Dance Every Night—Earl Adams' All-Star Band")—while others bore names meant to evoke exotica, like the Jungle Temple, the Orient Tavern and the Camel Inn ("Look for the Sign of the Camel!"). The seemingly benign name of one roadhouse—the Green Mill—was actually a nod to shady speakeasy culture, achieved by borrowing the name of a notorious Chicago hangout frequented by the infamous Prohibition-era crime boss Al Capone. (Interestingly, that Green Mill boasted a wooden hatch behind the bar leading to an escape tunnel that went under the street and into an adjacent building, allowing Capone and his gang to elude the authorities whenever raided—a feature that one Bothell Highway joint, the Jolly Roger, has long been rumored to have also had.)

THE BLACK CAT

The Bothell Highway was becoming a great attraction for the mobile set—as well as a serious magnet for trouble. The Black Cat was a chicken dinner roadhouse (with a "dancing parlor") that opened in 1921 and began to receive unwanted coverage by the *Seattle Times* in 1923. The newspaper reported on the action there and gave publicity to "a special committee appointed recently by the Seattle Council of Churches," which had called "on the board of King County Commissioners to discuss the roadhouse situation." The *Seattle Times* began posing questions like: "Roadhouses—what, if anything, should be done about them? Should they be under

Top: Seattle's Black Cat roadhouse perched above Victory Way, in the Victory Heights neighborhood, March 1923. *Courtesy Northwest Music Archives.*

Bottom: Roaring Twenties couple and their jalopy outside the Black Cat, March 1923. *Courtesy Northwest Music Archives.*

Night Owl Visits Roadhouses
※ ※ ※   ※ ※ ※   ※ ※ ※
Seeks Jazz and Refreshments

Tells About Convivial Parties, When Brunette Throws Salad at Singer and Girl of 20 Entertained by Man of 50.

Roadhouses—what, if anything, should be done about them? Should they be under stricter surveillance? Should they be abolished? Should they be permitted to operate as they now do?

It is not within the province of this article to attempt to answer these questions. But in this article, and subsequent ones, The Times, leaving its readers to form their own conjectures and seek their own answers, will present a picture of roadhouse conditions.

A mere narration of nightly occurences as viewed by a reporter in several of the roadhouses will be unfolded. Descriptions will be of the same degree of accuracy and realism that marked the "Saturday Nighter" articles which appeared in The Times last winter, depicting conditions in the city's public dance halls.

A special committee was appointed recently by the Seattle Council of Churches to call on the board of King County commissioners to discuss the roadhouse situation. Commissioners informed the committee last Wednesday that "because no specific complaint has been made," there would be no change in the policy of the board, allowing dancing after 1 o'clock in the morning. Yesterday, however, the commissioners reversed themselves and decided that roadhouses will be closed after 1 o'clock.

The Black Cat's nefarious activities were exposed by an undercover reporter from the *Seattle Times* on October 12, 1923.

stricter surveillance? Should they be abolished? Should they be permitted to operate as they do now?"

The newspaper sent an undercover reporter (along with a couple of companions) to check out the action. He hired a taxi and asked him "to recommend…a roadhouse where there would be both jazz and refreshments." His driver responded, "Yes, sir, there's the Black Cat on the Bothell Road.…If you want a good time that's a good place to go. You can get gin, Scotch or Canadian beer and I guess you don't have to be known." Upon arrival, our intrepid reporter was not exactly welcomed. A cook poked his head out and said they were closed, a sign on the piano inside read "Good Night" and a waitress informed him that "the liquor supply was exhausted." The reporter and his companion did, however, witness an inebriated customer loudly "singing something about Mammy, sweet potatoes and Alabama. He was off the key and couldn't remember all of the words." Observing that Mr. Birge's tavern—which would burn down on July 27, 1935—"had not the air of liveliness that we had expected," the reporter noted the manager had explained that this was a result of the "psychological effect among patrons" due to "the recent tragedy at The Grove, a roadhouse a mile and a half" up the road.

The Grove

When the *Seattle Times*' undercover reporter arrived at the Grove—which usually hosted boisterous crowds drinking and enjoying live jazz by Carroll's Famous Dance Orchestra every evening—he detected "a decided air of depression" about the place. No wonder. Several evenings prior, a freshly married young groom had been shot to death out on the veranda by a female stranger who had, according to the prosecutor, "taken many drinks of moonshine, gin and whiskey."

In reaction, the county prosecutor and sheriff proposed a "'clean-up' of all the roadhouses and chicken dinner inns in the county, where liquor is served and which operate all night." The resultant media frenzy disrupted all the usual fun. Looking across the "bare dance hall and the vacant orchestra chairs," the Grove's manager complained that his business had fallen off a cliff—"and they are making such a stir over it. Why, it could have happened in front of the Y.M.C.A. or any other place. We were running with a big business…until this happened. Now look at the place!" Denied drinks—even though the reporter noted that several of the very few customers in the joint "had with them bottles which the average person would find it difficult not to believe contained booze"—that particular evening's "fun" was over. Meanwhile, the sheriff "deplored the fact that so many 'chicken dinner' inns flourish. These places, he said, may be started by any one and operate without a license so long as they do not have dancing.…However, when they do hold dancing the roadhouses must obtain a license from the county commissioners." Yet even having a license didn't keep their troubles at bay.

The Blakehart Inn

Among the first of the chicken dinner speakeasies located along the Bothell Road, back in 1922, was Reese Blake and John G. "Jack" and Madge Lockhart's Blakehart Inn (at 11529 Twenty-Sixth Avenue Northeast). The inn boasted a large fowl mascot painted on the top front of the building—as did, evidently, most of these joints—and their slogan was "Watch for the Sign of the Blue Rooster." It was also advertised as being "close enough to the city to be convenient—far enough from the highway to lend an atmosphere of exclusiveness."

The Grove display ad promoting chicken dinners and Carroll's Famous Dance Orchestra. *The* Seattle Times, *January 24, 1923.*

The Grove faced the harsh glare of an investigative spotlight aimed by the *Seattle Times*, October 8, 1923.

The Lockhart Inn postcard, undated. *Courtesy Northwest Music Archives.*

The spot was "possibly the most intriguing speakeasy in the history of the…corridor, both because of its secrecy and its notoriety." Discreetly tucked away just west of the highway, it was, as once described by Vicki Stiles in the *Seattle Post-Intelligencer*, "a gated property with a long driveway leading to a building that looked a bit like a well-appointed farmhouse. It was listed as a private nightclub, and stayed out of the newspapers for many years, without even an advertisement to let people know it was in business."

Secret? Perhaps, but by the final years of Prohibition, law enforcement agencies had wearied of the place, and as the *Seattle Times* reported, one highway patrolman testified at a hearing in January 1932 that it was a "place where whiskey is openly poured, where drinking couples totter about on a tiny dance floor and where tipsy drivers start on drunken automobile joy rides." Within a week, the inn's license was revoked, but lobbying by the owners got the license reinstated in April. The Blakehart later morphed into the Lock-Hart Inn and then French's Inn, which featured nightly dancing to Johnny Chitwood's band and, of course, chicken and steak dinners. The building burned down in 1953, the target of a suspected arsonist thought to be responsible for the torching of numerous such amusement venues in the 1940s and '50s.

Parker's Bothell Highway Pavilion

It was in 1923 that a businessman named Roscoe F. "Dick" Parker (1892–1940) opened his Parker's Highway Pavilion (near Northeast 178th Avenue and the Bothell Road). The location he had selected was not accidental—it was adjacent to the My Southern Home restaurant, which had an "Orchestra Every Night" and also offered "chicken and steak dinners that will melt in your mouth." So the public was already aware that fun could be had at this bend in the road, and Parker's clientele would be able to avail themselves of the food offerings just across the way.

Also called the Bothell Dance Pavilion, the joint began drawing its own crowds way out here in the boonies by booking jumpin' dance bands—including Toots Bates and his Highway Pavilion Orchestra (who'd gained notoriety via their performances on Seattle's KFOA radio) and Barney's Jazz Band—to perform regularly at Parker's "large roomy dancehall." Trouble was brewing in the Parker household, though, and in 1929 the *Seattle Post-Intelligencer* noted that Dick's wife, Bessie, was granted a divorce due to his "habitual intoxication." News coverage noted that "other women" were involved in the matter and that he—"a wealthy meat market owner"—held half ownership in four butcher shops. She was ultimately granted custody of their two kids, and he moved. In 1930, Parker opened a second nightspot, Parker's Dance Pavilion, located a few miles west on the old Seattle-Everett Highway, and in 1935 he sold the Highway Pavilion.

The Green Mill

Located on the east side of the Bothell Highway just north of the city limits, this chicken dinner roadhouse was owned by Sarah Anderson, managed by Bill Lewis and featured a dance combo called Nebo's Big Three. But the Green Mill was a magnet for trouble throughout the 1920s—repeatedly getting busted for liquor violations as well as operating unlicensed dances. Indeed, the local newspapers took to calling those apprehended "jointists." The Green Mill's unsavory reputation was well known. "In a campaign against law violation, Sheriff Matt Starwich and deputies are making the roadhouses of the county objects of close scrutiny." The Mill was first raided on November 29, 1923, and both Anderson and Lewis were arrested for illegal possession of liquor: "Three quarts of whiskey, one quart of wine, and two quarts of

Dick Parker

Opens the

Bothell Highway

Pavilion

Saturday, May 23

Also

Sunday Night Dancing

With the

Popular

BARNEY'S Jazz Band

— My Southern Home —
Chicken Plate, 50c   Five-Course Chicken or Steak Dinner, $1.00
Home of the Famous Lemon Pie
On Bothell Highway
Orchestra Every Night   No Cover Charge Until After 10 P. M.

GALA OPENING!

DICK PARKER'S NEW

BOTHELL HI-WAY PAVILION

NEXT DOOR TO "MY SOUTHERN HOME"

JULY 3-4

Saturdays and Sundays Following

SUNDAY BARGAIN NIGHT

"Put" Anderson's Dance Band

Top: Toots Bates and his Highway Pavilion Orchestra, 1925, Seattle. Photograph by Hartsook Studios. *Courtesy Northwest Music Archives.*

Left: Dick Parker's Bothell Highway Pavilion grand opening display ad promoting Barney's Jazz Band. *The* Seattle Times, *May 23, 1931.*

Above: Dick Parker's Bothell Hi-Way Pavilion grand *re*opening display ad promoting "Put" Anderson's Dance Band. *The* Seattle Times, *June 29, 1934.*

NEW ROADHOUSE IS RAIDED, WHISKEY FOUND; 2 ARRESTED

SHERIFF'S deputies descended unexpectedly on the Green Mill, a new roadhouse on Victory Way, just outside the city limits, yesterday and, armed with a search warrant, inspected the place. Outside of the roadhouse, cached against the wall, they found one bottle of whiskey. In a bedroom they found another bottle of whiskey and a bottle of wine; in the ice chest, two bottles of beer and a bottle of whiskey. They arrested Mrs. F. Anderson, and B. Lewis, the manager. They were released on $500 bail each.

At Kirkland yesterday deputies arrested Vergil Foote and Lewis Nelson after purchasing a half gallon of moonshine with a marked $5 bill. Arrangements for the purchase were made with Foote and he received the money. When Foote and Nelson, who was with him in a small automobile, were arrested, the marked bill was found in Nelson's possession.

Left: Liquor raid at the Green Mill as reported by the *Seattle Times*, November 30, 1923.

Above: The Green Mill display ad promoting fresh chicken dinners and dancing to a "Five-Piece Ladies' Union Orchestra." *The* Seattle Post-Intelligencer, *April, 4, 1929.*

beer were found under a bed." Then on Christmas Eve 1923, one patron was arrested for having a bottle of whiskey under his party's table. Months later, on May 30, 1924, Anderson and Lewis were arrested again after a deputy sheriff discovered that they were running unlicensed dances. But this was still early in the Prohibition wars, and there would be more action here down the road.

McKenzie's Bungalow Inn (No. 1)

In June 1925, George W. McKenzie opened the Bungalow Inn roadhouse at the north end of Silver Lake up along the Bothell-Everett Highway. The resort included a ballroom—the Palace De Danse, which boasted a gigantic eight-thousand-square-foot maple dance floor and 2,700 blinking lights—with Barney's Bungalow Annex Orchestra, those "8 Masters of Jazz and Harmony," providing "the greatest music you ever heard." In addition, McKenzie featured his "famous Bungalow Inn Chicken Dinners." Alas, in mid-February 1929, the building was destroyed in a mysterious fire. This would not be the last of McKenzie's roadhouses to burn—a suspicious pattern that the *Seattle Times* would note led "Snohomish County and Federal officers" to investigate "the possibility that roadhouse racketeering may have been responsible for the blaze."

BUNGALOW INN

"The Daddy of Them All"

Steps another notch forward with its
Newest and Greatest Addition

PALACE De DANSE

Bungalow Inn Annex

It'll Surprise You
It'll Thrill You

8,000 feet of beautiful maple flooring, 2,700 myriad lights blinking, the
fantastic atmosphere of the dance swinging with the rhythm and melody
of the greatest music you ever heard—

Barney's Bungalow Annex Orchestra

8 Masters of Jazz and Harmony
featuring

Barney's Jazz Singing Trio

Dancing Every Saturday From 9:00 P. M. to 1:00 A. M.
Sunday, 7:30 P. M. to 11:30 P. M.

Popular Prices: Gentlemen, $1.10; Ladies, 25c (Tax Included)

Special Bungalow Chicken on toast 50c

Light Lunches and Refreshments Are Served Throughout Evening

The famous Bungalow Inn Chicken Dinners are Served as usual at the Inn
at $2.50 per plate, which entitles the guests to the courtesy of the Palace
de Danse for the evening. In other words, a chicken dinner as only The
Bungalow can serve it, and an evening of dancing that will thrill you with
its musical harmony, for five dollars per couple.

Located at the north end of Silver Lake, on the Pacific Highway,
just one hour's drive from Seattle.

GEO. W. McKENZIE
Owner and Manager

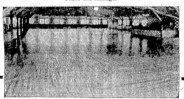

Top: Display ad for Geo. W. McKenzie's Bungalow Inn up at Silver Lake. *The* Seattle Times, *June 11, 1925.*

Bottom: Willard's Inn's "not a road house" debut display ad, February 1924. *Courtesy Northwest Music Archives.*

Willard's Inn

The increasingly sketchy reputation of the chicken dinner joints along the Bothell Highway had reached the point by 1924 that when a new one, Willard's Inn, opened for business (at Northeast Eighty-Ninth and the Bothell Road) "Just North of the Welcome Arch on the New Bothell Highway," it was marketed specifically as being "Not a Roadhouse." Clinton G. Willard's namesake restaurant/dance hall was proudly advertised as providing its clientele "clean fun at all times, with a close attention to law and order." There was great excitement when Willard installed a new music-making machine made by the Magnola Talking Machine Company of Chicago, and he sprang for large graphic ads in the newspapers to tout this entertainment addition. Willard hired a deputy sheriff as his doorman and touted the place as having "largest dance floor in the West," where the Tex Howard Orchestra (who would later become recording artists with the big-time Decca Records label) served as entertainment. In 1927, the place was advertised as Willard's Dancing Pavilion, featuring the "wonderful music of Ed Carey's Arcadians."

The Plantation/The Manor

In addition to his inn, Willard also ran the nearby resort the Plantation (at 14540 Bothell Highway), which was later rebranded as the Manor and featured "Southern Fried Chicken & Steaks Served in the 'Glorified' Manor," plus "THE BEST in Dining and Dancing" to music by El Arseneau and his orchestra. Times got tough, though, and Willard ended up filing for bankruptcy in June 1927—with the *Seattle Times* snarking in its news coverage that the place was "pretentious." By February 1928, the place was recast by Carl Marino—and his wife, Madame Katrino Marino (a coloratura soprano who sang for their guests)—as Marino's Café. By late 1930, it had reopened as the Terrace Gardens, and on January 11, 1931, federal Prohibition agents raided the joint just prior to a testimonial dinner honoring retiring King County commissioner William Brown. When the agents searched the premises and all parked cars, they found no liquor, but the happy event was spoiled. The following year, the business was transformed into the Tally-Ho Inn; then George W. McKenzie acquired it and renamed it McKenzie's Plantation. One year later, on July 4, 1933, the building burned to the ground. The site is now home to the Metro Heated Storage Building.

THE JUNGLE TEMPLE (NO. 1)

Announcing
the Opening of

The Jungle Temple

Wednesday Evening, July 22

NOT a chicken dinner inn; not a dance pavilion—a West Indian Jungle Temple.

Tropical dishes cooked by native chefs or old-fashioned American chicken dinners.

Or come and dance to the tantalizing strains of Hal Bellis and his Jungle Temple Orchestra.

Two miles north of the city limits, on the Bothell Highway, at 132nd St. and Victory Way. Reservations by phone.

FEATURING
New Orleans Chicken Gumbo and Jungle Rice

No Cover Charge

The Jungle Temple's grand opening display ad: "NOT a chicken dinner inn; not a dance pavilion." No, not at all…but come enjoy the New Orleans Chicken Gumbo and dance the night away! *The* Seattle Times, *July 22, 1925.*

On the evening of July 22, 1925, the Jungle Temple—located "at Williams' Grove on the Edmonds Road" (e.g., at 132nd Street and Victory Way)—held its grand opening. Just as Willard's Inn down the road had done, the owners initially made attempts to distinguish the Jungle Temple from the chicken dinner resorts that had been receiving so much negative news coverage. Indeed, the venue's very first advertisement announcing its arrival stated: "NOT a chicken dinner inn; not a dance pavilion." Instead, it was conceived as a "West Indian Jungle Temple"—albeit one that, in fact, offered patrons "old-fashioned American chicken dinners" along with "tropical dishes cooked by native chefs." And while perhaps not, somehow, a dance pavilion, it did invite customers to "come and dance to the tantalizing strains of Hal Bellis and his Jungle Temple Orchestra." Good intentions sometimes prove inadequate to temptations, and before long the Temple—which came to be popularly referred to as the "Jungle Inn"—would find itself under the scrutiny of the law.

Chapter 4

THE BIG BOTHELL HIGHWAY CRACKDOWN OF '27

While champagne corks were popping on New Year's Eve 1926, two federal Prohibition agents joined about one hundred revelers at Walter R. Rice's chicken dinner joint, the Camel Inn (formerly the Grove). But instead of partying along in the wee small hours, they were just surreptitiously observing the action. Then, "just when the hilarity was at its height…the agents revealed themselves, after spending several hours in the roadhouse, consternation reigned among the patrons." The agents' report stated that "frightened diners smashed bottles of liquor on the floor and against walls, doing such good execution that only a dozen were left intact for the agents to seize." Rice was arrested and all his "hysterical" patrons sent home.

One week later brought another big raid: "Sorrow knocked on the doors of two roadhouses on the Bothell Highway…when federal prohibition agents raided the two places and seized most of the fixtures. The raid on the Orient Tavern resulted in the reported seizure of 100 quarts of beer and twelve cases of alleged fake bonded whisky. Gillie Richardson, fifty-four, negro, said to be the owner of the roadhouse, was held on a charge of violating the federal liquor act. At the Jungle Inn, R.V. Owen, twenty-seven, negro, is said to have been caught in the act making a delivery of moonshine….Owen said he was the brother of the owner."

Then just a month later, on the night of February 5, 1927, Sheriff Claude G. Bannick and his deputies made a surprise "inspection tour" at fifteen different "resorts" along the Bothell Road—or what the *Seattle Post-Intelligencer*

RUM RAID ENDS IN FREE FIGHT

Merrymaking guests and a raiding party of Sheriff Claude G. Bannick's deputies "mixed it" in a lively free-for-all rough-and-tumble fight in the Jungle Inn early yesterday during a cleanup of Victory Highway roadhouses. Combatants emerged with more or less tattered clothing, bruised ears and noses and battered skulls.

Five highway resorts where revelry was in full swing were raided by deputies, and seven guests arrested. They were lodged in the county jail, charged with unlawful possession of liquor, in lieu of $750 bail each.

Incensed over the intrusion of the deputies, patrons of the Jungle Inn left their tables and rushed the raiders as they entered, endeavoring to put them out. A general melee ensued. Lew Fields and Tom Diffley, who, it is said, had brought a small quantity of liquor, were arrested.

At the Dixie Inn the raiders arrested C. Hoffman and C. Richardson; at Bob's Place, Fritz Sutter; at the Green Mill, James Sullivan, and at the Camel Inn, James Wilson.

The *Seattle Post-Intelligencer* reports on July 18, 1927, about a major multi-venue liquor raid along the "Bottle Highway."

described as "Seattle's Saturday night mecca of high jinks and revelry." One patron was arrested for liquor possession at My Southern Home, one at the Jungle Temple and one at the Toot Inn, as well as one waiter at the Camel Inn. Both Walter Rice and W.A. Newman, "negro" proprietor of the Tip-Top Inn, were instructed to report to the police station first thing Monday morning to explain why they were still open after one o'clock in the morning. Bannick was quoted saying, "My men did a good night's work in cleaning up. This is going to be a regular business until the Bothell Highway—or the Bottle Highway—whichever one wants to call it, is as dry as the Sahara."

Two months later, on April 3, 1927, Bannick's posse was hot on the trail again, and the *Seattle Post-Intelligencer* had its fun reporting the news. "Drys Mop Up Road Houses—'Blotter Squad' Finds Evidence of Moisture While Visiting Bothell Highway Resorts," ran the headline of a story recounting Bannick's arrest of three, including one at the Jungle Temple. On June 7, an ad offering the Tip-Top Inn as available for lease first appeared in the classified section—but that was presumably a tough sell given the zeitgeist of that era.

Five weeks later, on July 17, 1927, another big raid on five roadhouses was launched: two men were arrested at the Dixie Inn and one each at Bob's Place, the Camel Inn and the Green Mill. By this time, ownership of the Green Mill had changed, and its latest proprietor, W. Langer, was charged with six recent incidents of selling booze to undercover agents.

But it was at the Jungle Temple that the real action took place: "Merrymaking guests and a raiding party of…Bannick's deputies 'mixed it' in a lively free-for-all rough-and-tumble fight in the Jungle Inn early yesterday during a cleanup of Victory Way roadhouses. Combatants emerged with more or less tattered clothing, bruised ears and noses and battered skulls.…Incensed over the intrusion of deputies, patrons of the Jungle Inn left their tables and rushed the raiders as they entered, endeavoring to put them out. A general melee ensued." Two men were arrested for possession.

The pressure continued in October 1927 when deputy sheriffs made a string of raids at various Bothell Highway joints. Walter Rice, age twenty-nine, was arrested at his Camel Inn for selling liquor to the deputy sheriffs. Andrew Otto was arrested for possession of gambling devices at Otto's Place. And Henry W. Lemm was arrested for possession of liquor with intent to sell at Henry's Watermelon Palace. When they were all sentenced on December 14, the newspapers noted that "it was a hard day in the courts yesterday for Bothell Way roadhouses," as a jury returned a guilty verdict in the jointists' cases. Days later, on December 24, a prosecutor announced that he would be for the first time invoking the Volstead Act "giving state officials power to abate places in which liquor is sold"—"abate" being a legalistic word for "shut down." Later that day, a judge placed a restraining order on the Camel Inn and a couple other joints around town, in an act described in this way: "The first gun in the prosecutor's war for the abatement of alleged liquor joints was fired."

Doc Hamilton's Barbecue Ranch (No. 1)

The business empire founded by "Doc" Hamilton expanded when in 1927 he opened two new identically named roadhouses on the outskirts of town. The first was the Barbecue Ranch on the Bothell Highway, right near Mammy's Shack, and the second was the Barbecue Ranch over on Highway 99. (More about that in chapter 6.) At both nightspots, the high-profile proprietor managed to bring trouble with him. In January 1928, Hamilton was hauled into court to face charges that he'd been stiffing the American Oriental Cab Company, which won a judgment regarding his failure to pay them for providing transportation for his waiters to the Barbecue Ranch. Then in April a federal attorney brought changes against Hamilton that described his roadhouse as a "common nuisance where the national prohibition laws are violated." Abatement proceedings were filed in federal court with a goal of padlocking the joint.

One year later, a case against Hamilton—and a pair of dancing singers named Charles and Effie Tyrus—made a bit of legal history. On June 27, 1929, federal judge George M. Bourquin ruled that, as the *Seattle Times* noted, under general conspiracy statues, "musicians and entertainers in roadhouses, cafes and other places where the Volstead Act is violated are equally guilty with the proprietors of such places in encouraging and maintaining a nuisance under the liquor laws, and are also subject to criminal prosecution." Bourquin wrote, "Thus the defendants had a part in keeping up the nuisance and in supplying entertainment to facilitate it. They knowingly and intentionally countenanced and encouraged it, and joined in making that whoopee which favored the nuisance." The *Seattle Times* concluded, "This is the first time the Volstead Act has ever been construed by a court, fixing the status of entertainers in places where liquor is sold, and established a precedent to guide the enforcement officers in future activities."

The ever-wily Hamilton, however, once again managed to elude easy comeuppance, and his travails continued. On November 19, 1929, a new court trial before Judge Bourquin began. The prosecution, seeking abatement once again, relied on testimony from a "score of federal prohibition agents," who declared "that they visited the Ranch at various times over a period of several months, taking names of patrons and waiters, and making notes of liquor sales." On and on this dance continued, and Hamilton would find himself in court countless times—for infractions in town at the Barbecue Pit and also at his Barbecue Ranches on the Bothell Highway and over on Highway 99. (More about that in chapter 6.)

Chapter 5

AT THE CROSSROADS

In the early 1930s—during what would be the final years of Prohibition—a couple notable joints that would offer chicken dinners and live music opened for business at a key intersection along the Bothell Highway. Situated almost literally across the road from each other—and within seed-spitting distance of Henry's Lemm's Watermelon Palace—the Jolly Roger roadhouse and the regrettably named, and themed, Coon Chicken Inn were wisely built exactly where Twentieth Avenue intersected the highway. And Twentieth was a mainline street that aimed straight north from the University of Washington's Greek Row, making it a favored route for hordes of frat rats and sorority sisters who went out seeking fun on Friday and Saturday nights in their jalopies.

The Coon Chicken Inn and Club Cotton

The Coon Chicken Inn "resort" (at 8500¼ Bothell Way) opened in Seattle in August 1931, with Black waiters serving their popular thirty-cent "Coon Fried Chicken Sandwich," or "Coon Fried Steak" as well as chicken and steak dinners. Lester Graham had launched his restaurant chain back in 1925 in Utah, and eventually he added additional outposts in Portland, Spokane and Seattle. Graham's use of offensive graphic imagery—the chain's logo, a cartoon caricature of a winking Black bellhop, appeared on the inn's signage, menus, plates and even the main entrance itself—quickly brought a response from Seattle's burgeoning Black community.

Two weeks after the inn's grand opening, one of Seattle's Black-oriented newspapers, the *Northwest Enterprise*, published breaking news: "Citizens Protest Against 'Coon' Chicken Inn." Three days later, on September 21, 1930, the *Seattle Times* filled in more details: "A delegation of three negroes led by attorney Clarence Anderson protested...the use of the word 'coon' in the name of the inn....The delegates [said that] they are set up to ridicule through the name of the inn." Anderson was joined by two other Black leaders: William H. Wilson, president of the Seattle NAACP and editor of the *Northwest Enterprise*, and Horace R. Cayton, a prominent local civil rights advocate and newspaperman who was born on a plantation in Mississippi back in 1859. Their demand of the Grahams was that the inn cease its advertising mode or be charged with libel and defamation of a race. This confrontation continued, with other citizens also getting involved—and the *Times* also reported that "special police protection has been ordered on the Coon Chicken Inn...after [the] wife of the proprietor, complained...that she had received bomb threats."

In time, the Grahams agreed to tone things down—an agreement that they basically reneged on, and the inn carried on with its questionable ways. On February 21, 1934, a new nightclub opened in a newly built basement space. The Club Cotton could accommodate 250 people; patrons danced to

Summer season begins for various Bothell Highway roadhouses, including Parker's Pavilion, the Lockhart Inn and the Jolly Roger "Dance Tavern." *The* Seattle Post-Intelligencer, *June 29, 1934.*

Above: The Coon Chicken Inn postcard, circa 1930s. *Courtesy Northwest Music Archives.*

Left: The Club Cotton's grand opening display ad. *The* Seattle Times, *February 18, 1934.*

Above: Chinese Castle roadhouse undated advertising card that notes dancing to the Chinese Castle Orchestra. *Courtesy Ron Edge.*

Left: Chinese Castle display ad. *The* Seattle Post-Intelligencer, *September 13, 1935.*

music initially provided by the Club Cotton Merrymakers. Over time, other dance bands would be featured there, including one led by former Vic Meyer dance band member Max Pillar, as well as Johnny Maxon's Orchestra and Joseph "King" Oliver's Orchestra. While a majority of Seattle's population didn't seem to have a problem with the racist overtones of the inn, they definitely hurt the Black minority. And trouble seemed to dog the inn: in March 1937, members of the Bartenders, Cooks, Waiters and Waitresses Union (BCWW), along with Musicians Union players, picketed outside the place for a week demanding that their unions be recognized. Even with such actions being taken against it, the Coon Chicken Inn persevered until late 1949, when Lester Graham finally dismantled the entrance and shuttered his restaurant. By 1970, a modern new building had been constructed on this site, and from then until 2016 it was the home of a Chinese restaurant, Ying's Drive-In. In November of that same year, it was recast by new owners as a beer-oriented business called the Growler Guys.

The Jolly Roger (Part i)

In 1933, Seattle's appropriately named architect Gerald Castle Field was hired by a general contractor, E.B. Fromm, to design eye-catching roadside-attraction-quality architecture for a new castle-like building on a lot located just north of the city limits (at 8720 Bothell Highway) along the Bothell Highway. The building's main attraction was a tall two-tiered tower on its northeast corner—a tower that would go on to inspire generations of speculation and rumors.

It was in 1934 that a Chinese-born chef named Henry Kingzy Wong opened his Chinese Castle here, offering beer, dining and dancing to the Chinese Castle Orchestra. The documentary record appears to show that by June, E.B. Fromm had stepped in, announcing that he was opening his own Jolly Roger Road House in the same building—presumably with plans to run the dance hall (and perhaps other related businesses) while Wong ran the tavern and restaurant. The Jolly Roger held a soft opening on June 30, 1934, offering "chicken and steak dinners for those who are hungry" as well as a "tap room…for those who are thirsty" and dancing to Bob Dale's Orchestra. Interestingly, in May 1935, the Washington Liquor Control Board lowered the boom, revoking Wong's beer license; by year's end, he was out, and Fromm was running the whole shebang.

The Jolly Roger Roadhouse, Seattle, circa 1930s. *Courtesy Ron Edge.*

Opposite, top: The Jolly Roger's "formal" (second) grand opening display ad. *The* Seattle Post-Intelligencer, *December 20, 1935.*

Opposite, bottom: Interior view of the Jolly Roger's dance floor, jukebox and stage, undated. *Courtesy Shoreline Historical Museum.*

Above: The Jolly Roger, undated. *Courtesy Shoreline Historical Museum.*

Right: The Jolly Roger menu, undated. *Brad Holden's collection.*

It was on December 20, 1935, that the Jolly Roger marked its "Formal Opening" by offering "Spring Chicken dinners for 50-cents!" plus music by Gordon Kilbourne's five-piece orchestra and "an elaborate floor show" headed by Lou Kay, "Seattle's Favorite Blues Singer," and featuring the Davies Sister dance team. The Jolly Roger was a pirate-themed venue with that prominent pink stucco tower—soon to be boasting a large menacing skull-and-crossbones flag—that not only grabbed the attention of motorists but also sparked a legend that it had once served as a lookout station for employees scoping out the horizon for liquor agents or the sheriff. Another persistent bit of urban lore maintains that there was also an escape tunnel in the basement that headed eastward, under the highway, and allowed the clientele to flee during a raid and hide in the woods or skedaddle right over to the Club Cotton. Other than remnants of a plastered-over archway down there, no other definitive evidence has yet surfaced to prove anything one way or the other. The historical timeframe, however, does not necessarily add up, as the building was constructed after the repeal of Prohibition. Granted, though, plenty of other roadhouses chose to provide guests with booze illegally smuggled from Canada, so that scenario remains a possibility.

By April 1936, Fromm had finally had enough, and he sold the enterprise to one Orville R. Cleveland, who placed it up for sale in June 1938. In April 1940, the business was again offered for sale. Then, for more than four decades, Orville and Nellie Cleveland ran the Jolly Roger on this site, providing their clientele evenings of fun dining, drinking and dancing.

Chapter 6

THE RISE AND FALL OF THE
HIGHWAY 99 ROADHOUSES

It was back in 1906 that the Washington State Highway Commission issued a report noting the desire for "an improved highway extending across the state from Blaine…to a point on the Columbia River." In 1910, planning then began to extend such a route—to be called the Pacific Highway—all the way down through Oregon and California and southward to the Mexican border. In time, government legislation, such as the Federal Highway Act of 1921, encouraged the creation of more local highway systems. In 1923, a plan was put in place for a more direct route from Seattle to Everett, and a new highway was constructed using the North Trunk Road, an old roadway that originally started out as a primitive and narrow dirt trail used by horses and wagons.

Work on this project began in 1925, and on October 15, 1927, the new Seattle-Everett Highway officially opened to traffic, representing a significant improvement over the longer and more dangerous Bothell Highway. This new and more direct route would become part of the Pacific Highway (later US Route 99) and would serve as the main artery leading northward from the city—until Interstate 5 finally superseded it in the 1960s. Beginning in the 1930s, certain sections of this roadway (in what is now the Shoreline area) would become known as Aurora Avenue—a nod to the aurora borealis skies to the far north.

But already back in the late 1920s, various businesses had begun opening along this newly paved route, including gas stations, restaurants and overnight lodges. Joining these was a string of boisterous and rowdy roadhouses—all eager to fulfill the public demand for liquor, gambling and risqué entertainment. But their open flaunting of Prohibition laws quickly made them the targets of local law enforcement. These Seattle-Everett Highway roadhouses had some distinct characteristics that set them slightly apart from their Bothell Highway counterparts. Many offered gambling, which included everything from traditional card and dice games to devices such as slots, pinball machines and punchboards. Another defining trait was the heavy amount of prostitution, complete with "guest cottages" or "traveler inns" conveniently located either next door or across the highway, where customers and their new dates could finalize their business transactions. This arrangement may have been the origin of the "no tell" motel (motor-hotel) phenomenon. To set the proper mood, several of these clubs also offered all-girl revues and "exotic dancers."

Several of the Highway 99 roadhouses had elaborate and fancy exteriors that offered irresistible curb appeal to passersby; however, the buildings themselves were often crudely constructed with scrap wood. As a result, most of these roadhouses represented major fire hazards, and in fact, many met their eventual demise by burning to the ground in a spectacular fashion. As local historian Betty Gaeng noted:

> Most of them had fancy fronts but they were only facades. The backs of the buildings were just rustic boards as a rule, and I can remember some were just unpainted wood. So many of them burned—because they were wood and not the stucco so many seemed to be made of when you saw them from the highway—and I always thought they were burned on purpose by the owners. Maybe I remember that from listening to my father and other law officers and fire department men talking about their suspicions. Anyhow, in those days, the fire departments were pretty rustic too, no fire hydrants, and no way to really fight the fires, so the buildings just burned to the ground. The old roadhouses were thrown together so fast, I am sure the wiring was not that good either.

These roadside inns were known for being particularly rowdy during the weekends, when people looking for a good time would drive up from Seattle. The sounds of clinking bottles, laughter and music could be heard filtering out onto the street, and the interiors of these roadside taverns were packed with local revelers enjoying themselves a night out. According to Gaeng:

> While the roadhouses were busy all week, they really rocked on Saturday night. On Sunday mornings my brothers and I would get up before church

The Everstate Pavilion, undated photo. *Courtesy Shoreline Historical Museum.*

*and walk up the highway to collect all the bottles discarded by the side of
the road. We'd bring them back to Middleton's Store and cash them in for
the deposit, which we often spent going to the movies.*

This stretch of Everett Highway roadhouses reigned supreme throughout
the 1930s and '40s, though most had disappeared by the 1950s. The
roadhouses noted in this chapter represent the eclectic collection of
barrooms, gambling parlors and dance joints that inhabited this new
roadway. They ranged from small rustic taverns to big glitzy nightclubs
with music, dancing and live floor shows. Many were disreputable places—
inhabited by a colorful cast of characters—that represented over two
decades' worth of salacious newspaper stories, voluminous police reports
and unsavory personal anecdotes. Four of this area's earliest roadhouses
were the Everstate, McKenzie's new Bungalow Inn, the Jungle Temple and
Doc Hamilton's Barbecue Ranch.

THE EVERSTATE PAVILION

The grand opening event for the Everstate Country Club/Pavilion (at 12054
North 122nd Street and Fremont Avenue North) on May 2, 1924, attracted

an impressive five hundred guests. Although its golf course was still being planned, the clubhouse/ballroom was ready for action. Over the following years, the BYOB dances held there—until two in the morning—continued to bring the crowds, to the extent that in September 1928, fifty nearby neighbors signed a petition and "appeared before the Board of County Commissioners…in request that the dance license of the club be revoked on the ground that 'wild' and noisy parties are held on the property." Two days later, however, it was reported that even after "deputy sheriffs and a large number of residents of the district" testified "in strong terms," the Everstate's license was renewed.

By 1929, Tucker's Everstate Dance Band was gigging there, as well as performing live on KOL radio, and the room began advertising its dances with the slogans: "Ever step at the Everstate?" and "Take Your Date to the Everstate." In the early years of World War II, the club began an ad campaign that took into account the public's sense of wartime shortages and its effect on consumer costs: "$1/2$ Gallon of Gas to Everstate from City Center." By the 1930s, Gant Kuhn's Radio Band was playing there. During the '40s, bands playing there included the Center Case and His Orchestra, El Arsineau and His Orchestra, Top-Hatters, Kay Fox and His Orchestra, Henry Bickler's Orchestra, Bill Hadley's Band, Dave Williams' Band, Art Hollingsworth's 9 Royal Guardsmen, Allen Clark and His Orchestra, Viv Mayfield and His Lamp Lighters and the Sophisti-Cats. By 1950, other dance orchestras led by the likes of Milo Hall, Gordon Kilbourne, Frankie Roth and Max Pillar were playing the Saturday night gigs—but the Everstate's days were numbered.

McKenzie's Bungalow Inn (No. 2)

The first roadhouse known to operate on what would eventually become the "new Everett Highway" was McKenzie's Bungalow Inn, which had its official grand opening on October 30, 1926. Its exact location remains unknown, as it was never assigned an official address. Contemporary newspaper ads simply describe the location as being "at the end of the brick pavement on North Trunk Highway," though its listed phone number (Edmonds 8024) tells us that it was located somewhere on the Edmonds stretch of the new roadway.

George W. McKenzie's latest roadside resort was one of the more elegant clubs to exist north of the city. The advertisement for its grand opening

Full-page ad announcing the grand opening of McKenzie's Bungalow Inn. *The* Seattle Post-Intelligencer, *October 28, 1926.*

described the interior as having "a spacious ballroom with maple floor. Above, a glass ceiling, though which the most startling lights will throw their varied gleams…around the ballroom are nineteen cozy private dining rooms, each with its own cheery, heart-warming, glowing fireplace." Illustrations of McKenzie's Bungalow Inn confirm that it was a large, round, bungalow-style building with a series of fireplaces circling its palatial roof. Its motto was "where the searchlight throws its beam," as a giant spotlight in front of the building would help local merrymakers navigate toward its remote location.

Despite the inn's ostentatious façade, all varieties of illegal vice were widely available inside McKenzie's Bungalow Inn, which soon attracted the attention of local law enforcement. On December 31, 1927, as drunken revelers welcomed the New Year, its doors suddenly burst open and a large procession of sheriff's deputies marched in. Several other roadhouses were also raided that night, resulting in a record number of arrests. It would be the first of many such police visits until, finally, on March 2, 1929, deputies and federal agents conducted a large-scale raid—one of the largest ever conducted along Highway 99—in which over 150 people were rounded up and arrested on liquor and gambling charges, including McKenzie himself. Three days later, on March 5, his establishment suspiciously caught fire and burned to the ground. It is worth remembering that McKenzie's other Bothell Highway club, the Bungalow Inn, had also burned down in a very similar manner just a month prior. Soon after the raid, McKenzie was charged with an assortment of gambling charges and was sentenced to two years at the state penitentiary in Walla Walla. After his eventual release from prison, McKenzie took over ownership of another roadhouse on the Bothell Highway that was once known as the Plantation and renamed it McKenzie's Plantation. When that burned in 1933, it was McKenzie's third roadhouse lost to fire.

THE JUNGLE TEMPLE (NO. 2)

From the moment it opened in November 1927—with music provided by the Jungle Temple Orchestra, and/or Oscar Holden's 6-Piece Jazz Orchestra (with Miss Zelma Winslow, soloist)—Fred Owen's Jungle Temple was the host to more police raids than perhaps any of the other Highway 99 roadhouses. The nightclub had originally operated on the Bothell Highway, but eventually moved its operations to the new Everett Highway, on what is now the corner of 224th Street and Highway 99—thus its designation as Jungle Temple No. 2. Like other roadhouses in the area, the Jungle Temple boasted a small bandstand and dance floor, with occasional musical performances by the Doc Hamilton Quartet.

Left: The Jungle Temple No. 2 menu cover, undated. *Courtesy Northwest Music Archives.*

Right, top: The Jungle Inn display ad promoting Sunday dinners—including pan-fried chicken—and dancing. *The* Seattle Times, *July 11, 1927.*

Right, bottom: The Jungle Temple display ad promoting Oscar Holden's Jazz Orchestra. *The* Seattle Times, *November 23, 1927.*

One month after its grand opening, the Temple was part of the same New Year's Eve police raid that took down other nearby roadhouses. This didn't slow down, though, with several other police raids taking place there over the next few years. In September 1928, a large-scale raid at the Jungle Temple resulted in the arrest of almost one hundred people on various liquor and gambling charges. During another memorable raid in December 1929, customers started fighting back when sheriff's deputies tried to shut the place down, resulting in a violent brawl. In the end, five customers and one employee were arrested.

By 1931, the Jungle Temple offered its patrons a menu created by chef William Graves, formerly with Doc Hamilton's Barbecue Ranch, as well as an Entertainers Revue every Sunday, featuring the comedian/dancer "Rooster" Jenkins, Sally "the Crooning Troubadour" Harper and "Music Sure to Set Your Feet Atingling" by Gerald Well's Hi-Hatters Band. The Temple managed to survive until 1934, when it was finally declared a public nuisance and had its front doors permanently padlocked. Its proprietors were charged with several liquor and gambling charges and were sentenced to two years at the Walla Walla State Penitentiary. In the mid-1940s, the club would reopen under new owners as the Jungle, with a new location at what is now 230th Street and Highway 99. By 1946, the Jungle had gone out of business for good.

Doc Hamilton's Barbecue Ranch (No. 2)

It was also in 1927 that one of the most fabled and notorious of all local nightspots emerged, with a story that spanned nearly three decades. Part of its ongoing mystique lies in its long and infamous existence, while part of it lies with the various people who inhabited this notorious location. It operated under a few different names, but to many folks, it was simply known as the Ranch.

The club's saga began when Doc Hamilton was released from jail in July 1927. Surveying his options, Hamilton realized that he would need to find new locations for his business endeavors. Many of his Seattle nightclub brethren were feeling the tightening squeeze of King County sheriff Claude G. Bannick, who had been closing all the roadhouses, speakeasies and gambling parlors that were operating in Seattle. Speaking to reporters, Bannick made his intentions quite clear: "We mean business and I want the roadhouse proprietors to know it! We'll have the roadhouses closed as menaces to public safety." As a result, many club owners began heading north of the city and setting up roadhouses along the two new stretches of highway. Not wanting to return to jail, Hamilton decided to follow suit and scouted out a couple of potential spots that were both ideally located a couple miles north of the King County line. One of his new establishments would be located on the Bothell Highway; the other would open on the new highway. Both were named Doc Hamilton's Barbecue Ranch, though the one on the Seattle-Everett Highway would have the most storied existence.

As the *Seattle Post-Intelligencer* observed: "In search of wider spaces in which to conduct his growing business, and for other reasons, John H. 'Doc' Hamilton of local darktown fame, has 'moved over' into Snohomish County, where he will open today a new 'barbecue ranch' just off the brick highway thirteen miles north of Seattle. For some years Hamilton has operated the 'Barbecue Pit' in somewhat cramped quarters on Twelfth Avenue, sometimes visited by raiding squads, both gambling and dry. He gained prominence when, as a defendant in the famous Olmstead liquor conspiracy indictment, he sat through the long trial asleep much of the time, only to be freed on a verdict of not guilty."

The Barbecue Ranch was located along the Edmonds stretch of the highway (on what is now 220th Street Southwest and Highway 99). The initial newspaper advertisement for its grand opening was very inviting, promising music by the Darktown Jazz Band as well as "Entertainment— Black Bottom, Buck and Wing Contest—You should see these girls strut. They know how!" Hamilton's Barbecue Ranch officially opened for business on August 6, 1927, and despite its remote location, it quickly established itself as a beacon of local debauchery. The Barbecue Ranch featured one of the region's largest billiard rooms and provided a full array of beer, wine and spirits; it was also known to produce its own brand of moonshine. Probably its biggest draw was the sheer amount of gambling that was available to its guests. Almost immediately, the Barbecue Ranch became one of the area's biggest draws. People would pile into their automobiles and drive up from Seattle, crossing the county line to enjoy an uninhibited evening of illegal entertainment. All this action was conducted so openly that newspapers felt the duty to note it. On November 14, 1927, the *Seattle Times* reported:

> *For some time it has been known that just outside the northern boundaries of King County, a group of roadhouses, a veritable Monte Carlo, have arisen to offer the parched and thrill-seeking residents of Seattle a wet and joyous playground. The places run dusk to dawn and the patronage is heavy.…In some of the places liquor is said to be sold "over the bar," and in others there are liquor "concessionaires" who deliver to the patron's automobile or table.…Seldom, even in the hectic heyday of Seattle's turbulent youth, were there resorts more openly conducted than are these outwardly dingy and inwardly gilded taverns.…Furtive men in high-priced automobiles are said to make furtive deliveries of wet goods to the kitchen doors of the taverns.*

Naturally, a continually packed nightclub with its large lighted sign out front beaming Hamilton's name and likeness did not go unnoticed by local officials, and plans for how to deal with this new public menace were swiftly put into place by the Snohomish County Sheriff's Department. Joining them in these discussions were members of the Prohibition Bureau, including assistant director William Whitney, who had previously brought down Olmstead's bootlegging operation. With Olmstead now in prison, Hamilton

Doc Hamilton's Barbecue Ranch display ad for grand opening with music by the Darktown Jazz Band. *The* Seattle Times, *August 6, 1927.*

became Whitney's next big target, especially given that he had managed to avoid prosecution during the Whispering Wires trial.

Within a couple months of the Barbecue Ranch's opening, additional roadhouses also started popping up, including the notorious Jungle Temple No. 2. The sheriff's department discussed this new development with Prohibition officials, and a plan was put into place to jointly raid all known liquor clubs along this new stretch of highway. For maximum effect, one of the busiest nights of the holiday season was chosen as the date they would strike, and their first stop would be Doc Hamilton's place.

As 1927 drew to a close, many of these newly established, north-of-the-county-line roadhouses were proving to be especially popular New Year's Eve destinations for local revelers in search of a good time. The Barbecue Ranch would be one of the area's hot spots that night, as word about Hamilton's new club had quickly spread far and wide. By ten o'clock that evening, the place was packed with inebriated guests. Hamilton was not present, as he was likely tending to his club in Seattle. In his place was manager O.W. Owen, who would go on to boast one of longest and most impressive criminal rap sheets of all local roadhouse owners. This particular night would be Owen's first arrest, which took place at approximately fifteen minutes after midnight when a large procession of sheriff's deputies and Prohibition agents suddenly stormed through the front door of the Barbecue Ranch and, with guns drawn and badges held high, placed everyone under immediate arrest. There was a brief period of pandemonium as some guests tried to flee, but the sheer number of law enforcement officials prevented any escapes, and everything was swiftly shut down in a highly efficient manner. Five cases of liquor were seized, and Owen was arrested on federal liquor charges after admitting to being the one in charge. Joining Owen in the paddy wagon were all the club's employees, as well as several customers, including a prominent Seattle physician. Everyone was then taken to the Snohomish County Jail. A total of four other roadhouses were also raided that night: the Bungalow Inn, the Maryland Inn, the Jungle Temple No. 2 and the Olympic Tavern.

Immediately following the raid, the Barbecue Ranch was padlocked, and a few days later, William Whitney announced that he was seeking a federal abatement against Hamilton's place to make sure it never opened again. The case of the four other roadhouses raided that night was a bit different. As Snohomish County sheriff George I. Stever promised, "I don't think we have enough evidence.…But I figure on 'riding' them just the same. I'm getting tired of the way they are carrying on, but so far we haven't had enough luck in our raids on them."

Down in King County, Sheriff Bannick trumpeted news of the raids: "I've got the roadhouses on my side of the line pretty well regulated, but our work has been hampered greatly by the resorts flourishing just across the line. There's no question about the highways becoming far, far safer if the lid goes on these places and stays put!"

To get around this, Hamilton sold the Barbecue Ranch to manager O.W. Owen. This change in ownership allowed the club to legally avoid abatement and gave Hamilton a quick and easy way out. To his way of thinking, the New Year's Eve raid was an obvious sign that he was in the crosshairs of all local law enforcement, thereby making it impossible for him to run a successful business along either of these new highways. After all was said and done, Doc Hamilton owned the Barbecue Ranch for only about five months before he was forced to sell out. Its new owner, O.W. Owen, would run the establishment for the next decade, during which it would continue to endure countless police raids and legal troubles.

On February 5, 1928, the club's reopening was announced to *Seattle Post-Intelligencer* readers in a small article titled, "All Is Merry at Doc Hamilton's Again." Even though Hamilton was no longer the de facto owner, the place was continuing to operate under its original name, and he would even make occasional "guest appearances" to help keep the brand name alive. Less than three weeks later, though, the Barbecue Ranch was once again raided by sheriff's deputies, and Owen was jailed on gambling charges and later released on $1,500 bail. The establishment was once again padlocked, and

Doc Hamilton's Barbecue Ranch, October 1927. *Courtesy Ron Edge.*

sometime later that year, a fire mysteriously broke out, and parts of the club were destroyed. Owen was somehow able to retain ownership and, in fact, oversaw a complete renovation of the building, in which its square footage was significantly expanded to include the addition of a bandstand and a large ballroom for dancing. In 1929, it would reopen for business with a new, shortened name: the Ranch.

Like its predecessor, the Ranch freely offered a smorgasbord of booze and gambling, as well as a row of "overnight cabins" that were conveniently located directly across the street. These nearby motels and lodges were a common feature of roadhouses along the new Everett Highway, in which women of a certain profession would make themselves known in the bar area, and any interested parties could then negotiate further transactions in these conveniently located overnight rooms. In most cases, the proprietor of the roadhouse would also be the owner of the adjoining motel. It was a clever way to operate a side prostitution business without anything illegal taking place inside the club itself. Local historian Betty Lou Gaeng grew up near Highway 99 during the 1930s and '40s, and she vividly remembers the roadhouses that dotted the landscape near her home—especially given that her father was a local deputy who was involved in several high-profile police raids. Gaeng recalled this about the notorious highway cabins:

While the roadhouses were notorious for connecting prostitutes with their customers, the "business end" of the transaction was typically conducted in a collection of motels and cottages, often conveniently located just across the highway....People wandered back and forth across the highway between the roadhouse and the cabins. Even though there wasn't a lot of auto traffic, at night it was dark, and there was a lot of alcohol consumed at the nearby night spots. Sometimes people crossing the street were hit by cars. Since we lived just north at 212th Street, my father was often the first law man on the scene.

Through it all, the Ranch was considered to have some of the best entertainment, food and liquor in the entire Northwest, and it became quite a popular venue. During its first year in business, the Ranch was raided twice by federal agents. During the second raid, which took place in October 1929, agents broke up a gambling game and seized some liquor, and Owen was once again arrested and hauled away to the Snohomish County Jail. Meanwhile, Hamilton was continuing to go through his own legal troubles, serving one hundred days in jail in the summer of 1929. Despite his imprisonment, he continued to receive accolades from the press, with the *Seattle Post-Intelligencer* describing the jailed restaurateur as "one of the most spectacular figures in Seattle's nightlife for the last decade."

Despite all the public praise, Hamilton's legal troubles continued to multiply. On May 25, 1931, his Barbecue Pit was raided once again by the King County sheriff's squad, and the following day the *Seattle Times* noted that he was also being sued by the New York–based American Society of Composers, Authors and Publishers (ASCAP) after someone ratted him out for singing a copyrighted song there. Hamilton—who occasionally fronted his own a capella vocal ensemble, the Doc Hamilton Quartet—complained that "Sheriff Bannick's

Doc Hamilton's Barbecue Ranch display ad. *The* Seattle Post-Intelligencer, *February 18, 1928.*

trying to send me 'up the river' and now someone else is suing me because I sang 'Old Man River' in my Barbecue Pit."

Between June and August 1931, a plainclothes Prohibition agent visited the Pit on three different evenings, in which he witnessed active drinking and inebriated dancers. As a result, several charges were filed against Hamilton, including that he was running a gambling racket in a back room. Then in March 1932, King County sheriff Harry Lewis raided Hamilton's club, resulting in even more charges. During his subsequent trial, Doc testified that the Pit's atmosphere resembled that of an old southern home. "We had barbecued meats and harmony singing and sometimes the guests would join in singing a chorus, but I never sold any liquor," he explained. "I'm sort of sorry for myself, but I'm being done an injustice as I warned folks they'd get into trouble if they brought liquor to the Pit." Well, perhaps, but there was plenty of eyewitness testimony that Hamilton understood he was regularly charging his clientele a fee for providing them with setups—glasses, ginger ale and cracked ice to make their own cocktails with. In the end, Hamilton was found guilty of being a "common gambler" and sentenced to an eighteen-month prison term at the Walla Walla State Penitentiary.

The Ranch matchbook, circa 1930s. *Brad Holden's collection.*

Perhaps the only upside to all this turmoil, according to the *Seattle Times*, was that "while Doc Hamilton is on vacation, his piano player, Oscar Holden, has more time to practice." Holden was a key figure on the scene—and can be considered the "Father of Seattle Jazz." He'd arrived in Seattle at the dawn of the Roaring Twenties, playing clarinet along with his bandmate, the legendary boogie-woogie pianist (and self-described "Inventor of Jazz") Ferdinand "Jelly Roll" Morton. Jelly Roll eventually split, while Holden went on to entertain locals for decades and sire a brood of musically gifted kids who would help found the Northwest's early R&B scene.

Meanwhile, the Ranch's program of illicit entertainment continued well into the 1930s,

The Ranch "Seattle's theatre café" postcard, 1940. *Courtesy Northwest Music Archives.*

though this certainly did not go unnoticed by law enforcement. Owen, who also simultaneously operated a few other nearby clubs, amassed power in his new role and for several years served as the unofficial boss of the Highway 99 roadhouse scene. But even that status couldn't keep the law off his back. Snohomish County sheriff Walter E. Faulkner and his deputies raided the Ranch twice in late 1931, without any luck in finding evidence of liquor violations. But then, on the evening of December 6, 1931, five undercover dry agents entered the Ranch, mingled with the boozy crowd, took notes and, at one in the morning, were joined by six additional agents. Their mission that night was enforcement of the so-called hip flask provisions of the Volstead Act, as a new trend had emerged among roadhouses in which liquor was smuggled in by the guests themselves rather than being served by the establishment. It was all just a surreptitious way to keep the party going. As a result of the undercover stakeout that night, seven patrons were arrested for bringing flasks full of booze into the club. The next day, the head of the local Prohibition office announced that he was now enforcing the flask rule, causing the *Seattle Times* to offer this warning to potential roadhouse habitués: "Patrons of Roadhouses, night clubs and other rendezvous of drinking parties may expect arrest hereafter if they 'tote a flask.'"

Prior to this announcement, when revelers had been caught with a flask jammed in their waistband or pocket, it had been standard practice "to let state or city officers handle the flask cases" rather than bogging the Feds down with these more trivial arrests. But the flask fad had only grown as partiers figured out that carrying a flask was safer than buying a bottle from a roadhouse.

It was about this point in time that Doc Hamilton's Barbecue Pit was recast as the 908 Club and then, on October 19, 1932, Prohibition agents and sheriff's deputies raided the Pit and seized a whopping two ounces of gin, which led to new abatement proceedings against the joint. As Betty Lou Gaeng wrote about this:

> *His career of breaking the law was over when his Seattle club was raided by a King County sheriff with a much sterner idea regarding the law. Doc Hamilton was charged with the federal crime of bootlegging and sentenced by a judge to five years in a federal prison. This was considered very severe punishment.….No white prohibition club owner up to that time had ever received such harsh treatment.*

While he was imprisoned, Hamilton's properties—including his beloved European-style villa at 417 Twenty-Ninth Avenue East in the Madison Valley neighborhood—were confiscated and sold off. In April 1933, the 908 Club resurfaced as the Mardi Gras with Joe Adams's ten-piece as the house band, and then in 1934, it was recast again as the Auto Social Club. By 1935, it was called the Town Pump. That April, it was raided by state liquor inspectors five times within two days, and nearly fifty dancing patrons were arrested on liquor charges. In 1936, it changed names again, this time becoming the Bagdad. Over subsequent decades, this was the site of a series of restaurants and was recast once again as an Irish joint, the Chieftain Pub, in 2011.

When national Prohibition was repealed in 1933, Owen tried to steer the Ranch into more of a legitimate dance-and-dine entertainment venue. Instead of a roadhouse, it now billed itself as a "suburban cafe." Owen tried to shed his reputation as a shady nightclub owner and become more of a respected impresario. The Ranch began holding nightly revues, where guests could enjoy a fancy dinner while watching an elaborate floor show that featured an eclectic mishmash of dancers, musicians, comedians and entertainers. A large dance floor allowed guests to foxtrot and Lindy Hop during the musical numbers. However, the Ranch's reputation preceded it, and Owen found it difficult to shed the club's past entirely. Not to mention that a quick game of poker or blackjack was an easy way to help generate some extra revenue on those especially slow nights. And if some of the guests wanted to enjoy a drink or two while playing cards, then whose place was it to ruin their fun? Meanwhile, after serving only ten months in prison, Hamilton was pardoned on September 8, 1933, and released on parole on December 21.

By the mid-1930s, the Ranch had gradually devolved into its original form. The nightly dinner cabaret continued, but so did the drinking and gambling, which the police were more than ready for. In July 1935, Owen was arrested for running a gambling operation at the Ranch. A roulette wheel was said to be spinning when police arrived. On January 24, 1936, police conducted another late-night raid and seized twenty-five bottles of liquor. The next day, the sheriff's department ordered that the Ranch's entire bar be confiscated, and a furniture van pulled up and hauled everything away.

Undeterred, the Ranch opened a second dance floor known as the Royal Purple Room in the summer of 1936. There were now two dance floors, each with its own big band orchestra. The Ranch could now accommodate up to five hundred patrons, and it frequently did, with two different floor shows happening at the same time. Owen made sure that liquor was still available to those who wanted it, and in December 1936, he was once again arrested by WSLCB agents for violating the Steele Act. This would be Owen's final arrest.

The Ranch postcard (undated) showing the exterior, dance floor and bandstand. *Courtesy Northwest Music Archives.*

At the beginning of 1937, Owen began sponsoring a football team as part of the Seattle Community Football League. They were known as the Ranch Eleven. He continued operating the Ranch as one of the area's most popular "dinner theaters," and despite his many arrests, had positioned himself as one of the region's top club owners. For a person who started out as a young barkeep for various Seattle saloons, he had made quite a name for himself, managing to earn some actual respect as a local impresario. Sadly, this all came to end on December 19, 1937, when Owen was killed in a head-on collision.

That fateful day started out as any other, with Owen heading out in his car for a morning of local errands. He was driving southbound on Aurora Avenue when he noticed another car in the opposite lane suddenly veer over and begin driving straight toward him. Owen instinctively steered his car over into the shoulder to avoid being hit, but the other car was driving at too fast a speed, leading to a direct collision. It was such a powerful crash that both drivers suffered significant injuries and were taken to the nearby Providence Hospital. The other car was driven by a young college student named Alexander S. Ballinger, of the prestigious Ballinger family. He reported to police that he had just attended a minstrel show at the University Club and had drunk some champagne. His father was a prominent Seattle attorney, and his uncle happened to be Richard A. Ballinger, who was mayor of Seattle from 1904 to 1906, followed by a term as secretary of the interior under the William Howard Taft administration. Nearby Lake Ballinger was named after the family, and to say that they carried a tremendous amount of power and influence would be an understatement.

Nine days later, Owen died as a result of his injuries. He was forty-nine years old. Despite eyewitness testimony that Ballinger was "under the influence of intoxicating liquors and driving in excess of seventy-five miles per hour," he was never charged with a crime, though Owen's widow, Wanda Owen, later filed suit against the Ballinger family and won a $12,500 settlement. It was never explicitly explained how Ballinger escaped any legal repercussions, though his family connections certainly did not go unnoticed. For some, Owen's death carried a certain level of karmic irony, as there had been several well-known automobile fatalities resulting from drivers leaving the Ranch in an impaired state. Later that summer, in an act that could be seen as redemptive, Ballinger saved a couple from drowning after their sailboat capsized in nearby Lake Washington.

Doc Hamilton's fate was also marked by unfortunate circumstances. By 1935, he was running a rural farm called Berrydale outside of Kent. On

July 18, he ran a newspaper ad that stated: "Doc Hamilton Invites all his friends and former patrons to a Free Barbecue—All night Saturday and all day Sunday at his farm—Come and Bring Your Appetite." But even that fun would come to a notable end when on July 1, 1936, Hamilton and his farm truck were involved in a traffic accident—or rather, two. Appearing in court to face charges of reckless driving, Hamilton told the judge that the first incident occurred when another driver hit his truck with their car. It was later that Hamilton had collided with the Montlake Streetcar at Seattle's Twenty-Third Avenue and East Madison Street. The streetcar driver insisted that Hamilton had been drunk, to which Doc countered, "I wasn't drunk....I was just fighting with my wife." He also freely admitted, "There are just two things I shouldn't do. One is driving that truck of mine and the other is farming. I've quit both."

But Hamilton couldn't quite quit the nightlife; by New Year's Eve 1936, he was back at the site of his old Barbecue Pit (now called the Bagdad), and advertisements beckoned patrons to come and "Meet Doc Hamilton— Taste His Southern Dishes—Enjoy His Harmony." In 1939, Hamilton regained ownership of the business, but it eventually failed, which some of his associates attributed to "his own generosity." Hamilton died an impoverished and lonely death on September 8, 1942, in the Mar Hotel in Seattle's Chinatown neighborhood.

Following Owen's death, the Ranch continued to operate as before, though the number of police raids and arrests decreased substantially. Efforts were made by the new owners to clean things up and operate as a more legal and respectable nightclub featuring big band music that was popular during that era. As Betty Lou Gaeng recalls:

> *Back during the late 1930s and '40s, some like The Ranch were very popular and could afford good entertainers, so they attracted people with money—others were just so-so—probably didn't have big profits. Throughout the 1940s, ballroom dancing hit the high notes....Those were the days when a big night out was the dancing. The Ranch fell into that too and the vices of gambling and a lot of drinking kind of fell by the wayside...with the big crackdown on gambling at the roadhouses, mom and pop stores and taverns kind of took over the gambling—with the pull tabs in the 1940s. Those got very popular, and caused a lot of marital problems.*

Local entertainers, like the so-called Gentleman of Song, "Boob" Whitson, and his orchestra, were regular performers at the Ranch. Wyatt

Right: A happy John Henry "Doc" Hamilton, 1935, before his speakeasy empire crumbled. *Courtesy Northwest Music Archives.*

Opposite: El Rancho grand opening display ad. *The* Seattle Post-Intelligencer, *March 27, 1946.*

Howard was another veteran bandleader who played the Ranch several times. In a newspaper interview, Howard recalled being paid on "speakeasy scale" when playing at the Ranch, which was slightly higher than standard musician rates. And while the gambling had gone away, alcohol was still an important part of the experience, with many roadhouses now operating as "bottle clubs," where guests snuck in their own bottles of booze. The Ranch operated as a bottle club like the others but, in its attempt to rehabilitate its image, was much more low-key about this. As Gaeng notes, "World War II seemed to begin the change from calling them roadhouses to nightclubs."

In 1942, one of the Ranch's former co-owners opened an affiliate cabaret called the Town Ranch (at 1421 Eighth Avenue) in downtown Seattle, and it became a popular and legally run nightclub. But perhaps the biggest change for the Ranch occurred in 1946, when it once again changed ownership and reopened under its final name: El Rancho. It continued to run as a cabaret-style dinner club. A week before El Rancho's grand opening, a newspaper advertisement promised that "the lavishly-decorated club will feature exceptional cuisine in addition to top-flight entertainment garnered from all over the nation."

The nightly floor shows continued, as did the copious amounts of drinking, though on November 2, 1948, Washington State Initiative 171 was passed, which approved the sale of liquor by the drink, thereby giving licensed bars, restaurants and nightclubs permission to sell cocktails and hard liquor without risk of arrest. This spelled the official end of the bottle club era. The one caveat was that any establishment seeking to serve cocktails and mixed drinks was now required to obtain a Class H license, for which several strict requirements were expected to be followed—and once again, the WSLCB was tasked with enforcement. Probably the most impactful new rule was that any business operating with a Class H license needed to have a proper working kitchen in order to offer at least four "complete" meals. In addition, the WSLCB mandated that any taverns or nightclubs with a Class H license must not have any windows or open doorways, in order to prevent the general public from seeing hard alcohol being consumed. It wouldn't be until 1976 that the "no windows" rule would be lifted and daylight bars allowed to flourish once again.

In 1951, H.B. Neilson bought El Rancho and began offering "superb cuisine—prepared under the personal supervision of 'Blue Ribbon' Chef, Mr. Danny Beer," along with "smooth dance rhythm by Maestro Jack Otto and his 9-piece orchestra." As a result of changing music tastes, big band orchestras

became less popular, and El Rancho began operating more as a family restaurant than a nightclub. However, the establishment was never able to fully escape its checkered past, and on April 22, 1956, El Rancho was raided by Snohomish County deputies due to illegal gambling. One of its back rooms had been repurposed as a gambling hall used by a large-scale bookmaking ring that was said to be in active operation when police arrived. A total of twenty people were arrested, including several well-known "bookies." Deputies confiscated a large assortment of cash, gambling equipment, racing forms and ticket stubs. One of the most surprising discoveries was a dedicated phone line that secretly ran from El Rancho to an international gambling hub up in Victoria, British Columbia.

Three years later, in 1959, El Rancho began hosting nightly bingo games, which attracted an older and less rowdy crowd. Despite the improved temperament of its new clientele, bingo was still considered to be a form of illegal gambling and so El Rancho was prone to frequent visits by the Edmonds Police Department. The chief of the Edmonds Police Department, Rube Grimstad, gave several warnings to El Rancho to shut the bingo games down or else it would be closed down. On the night of May 28, 1959, the police chief paid one last visit to El Rancho to issue a final ultimatum: end the illegal bingo games or the police department would be shutting things down for good.

A few hours after Chief Grimstad's visit, the Edmonds Fire Department received a call that El Rancho was engulfed in flames. A total of seven fire trucks responded, but by the time they arrived, the entire building had been swallowed by fire and was well beyond the possibility of saving. It was windy that night, so the firemen instead focused their efforts on preventing the flames from spreading to other nearby buildings. By morning, all that remained of the historic nightclub was a smoldering pile of charred ruins. Despite a subsequent investigation by the local fire marshal's office, the exact cause of the fire was never determined, though the suspicious timing of it did not go unnoticed.

The loss of the building left a gaping hole in the local nightlife landscape, as it represented thirty-two years of drinking, dancing, gambling—and countless exciting police raids. Despite all the different owners and name changes over the years, the Ranch's dubious ending mirrored its illegal beginnings. To some, it was the sad end of a local landmark, though for many local residents, the general sentiment was "good riddance."

Rubenak's

Al F. Rubenak's roadhouse billed itself as a "theater supper club" that provided its clientele with bawdy entertainment for over two decades. Rubenak had previously used the building to run a restaurant called the Pig, but when Prohibition was repealed in 1933, he reopened as a roadside inn. Rubenak's offered the typical dining and dancing that was provided by many local clubs but was perhaps best known for staying open until four in the morning. Located on the east side of what is now Highway 99 and 188th Street Southwest, Rubenak's official motto was "Drink to the future and forget the past," and indeed, the booze flowed so freely at this well-known roadhouse that some partiers probably forgot what they did the night before.

Above: Rubenak's, circa 1930s. *Courtesy Alderwood Manor Heritage Association.*

Left: Rubenak's menu, circa 1930s. *Brad Holden's collection.*

Rubenak's was probably best known for its large, iconic sign out front depicting a waiter with a tray full of drinks. The sign was made by Walter A. Beebach (father of local historian Betty Lou Gaeng), who started out as a commercial artist in Seattle, then switched professions and became a Snohomish County deputy. Somewhat ironically, Beebach was involved in a police raid at Rubenak's in which he had to arrest the same people he had made the famous sign for. The club was the site of several police raids during its time as a roadhouse. In 1943, Al Rubenak—tired of all the legal hassles associated with the place—sold the joint and retired from the nightclub business for good.

The club continued to operate as Rubenak's, though, going through a series of different owners, habitually running afoul of the law, and thus being cited for numerous liquor and gambling violations well into the 1950s. In 1956, the *Seattle Times* sent one of its reporters to Rubenak's and found over one hundred customers sitting throughout the place and blackjack, craps and dice games being played in different rooms. Meanwhile, on the stage, music was reportedly provided by a clarinet player and a one-armed drummer, while three "scantily-clad" dancers entertained guests as part of their "girl revue." When asked for comment, a Seattle police officer quipped, "They sure run things differently in Snohomish County, don't they?"

Soon after the *Seattle Times'* expose, Rubenak's was finally shut down following a raid by the Snohomish County Sheriff's Department. It reopened later that year as Bill Easley's Supper Club. Advertisements for the new club indicate that it continued to operate as before with floor shows, mixed drinks and exotic dancers. This new club only managed to survive for a little over a year before it, too, was put out of business for good.

THE OASIS

The Oasis—a Prohibition-era slang word for a speakeasy—opened in 1931 and established itself as a "suburban cafe" along the new Everett Highway. Originally, the building had fairly plain architecture, but a few years after its opening, it was completely remodeled in an art deco style with towers and elaborate paneling added to the street side to create an enticing entrance. Inside, the Oasis boasted a large dining room that could seat five hundred people. In the center of the room was a dance floor, about thirty by ninety feet, surrounded by tables. At that point in the club's history, it became known for its nightly floor shows, and it billed itself as "the largest and finest suburban restaurant in the Pacific Northwest." A local newspaper described the establishment as "a popular rendezvous for after-dark entertainment seekers."

Like most highway resorts, the Oasis operated openly as a known bottle club yet somehow managed to avoid any of the high-publicity legal hassles that other roadhouses all seemed to endure. Menus from the Oasis confirm that it offered the standard setup found in most bottle clubs, including a pitcher of ice and a wide array of mixers such as ginger ale, lemon sour, sparkling water and lime rickey.

While the Oasis managed to avoid any legal trouble throughout most of its existence, its final few months saw the club engulfed in a mysterious scandal. The sordid tale began in January 1946, when it was announced in the papers that tax liens were being placed on the Oasis due to some outstanding debts that the owner had with the IRS. Three months later, on March 12, 1947, the Oasis burned to the ground after a suspicious fire broke out. The cause of the fire was never determined, but a year later, in June 1948, the owner suddenly went missing. At that point, he owned a new restaurant, which was also located on Aurora Avenue. He stopped by this new business on a Monday morning, told his employees that he was picking up the weekend's totals to deposit at the bank, then simply disappeared. He was married with five kids, and his distraught wife reported to newspapers that she was worried because he was known to have migraines, and she was concerned that such a headache may have caused him to get disoriented and become lost. A month later, authorities discovered him to be living in Phoenix, Arizona. He reported that he had amnesia and didn't remember how he got there, at which point some "truth serum"—a drug used to extract truth from suspects—was administered to him, which miraculously restored his memories. After having been being missing for a total of forty days, the fellow was reunited with his family, and apparently the rest of his life was spent controversy-free.

THE BLAKEWOOD INN

Opened in 1929 by O.W. Owen (who would also go on to run the Ranch), the Blakewood Inn almost immediately gained notoriety as the epicenter of neighborhood crime. Located on the southeast corner of what is now 212th Street and Highway 99, the inn was one of the more rowdy and violent

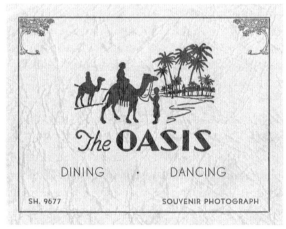

Top: Seattle's "Oasis Suburban Restaurant" postcard, 1937. *Courtesy Northwest Music Archives.*

Bottom, left: The Oasis souvenir photograph folder, April 1945. *Courtesy Northwest Music Archives.*

Bottom, right: The Oasis menu, circa 1940s. *Brad Holden's collection.*

roadhouses, a place known for making its own gin and for being a hot spot of robberies, gunfights and other illegal activity.

In one of its more memorable moments, a would-be robber entered the Blakewood Inn, pulled a gun on Owen—who was running the bar—and demanded money from the cash register. Owen responded by drawing a pistol from behind the counter and opening fire. A dramatic gunfight ensued, with the robber managing to escape in a car. The Blakewood Inn was also the site of a large-scale New Year's Eve raid in which sheriff's deputies arrested several people. Owen's other establishment, the Ranch, was also raided that night, as was the nearby McKenzie's Bungalow Inn.

The Blakewood Inn—whose interior boasted a small stage and dance floor with music provided by house band the Blakewood Syncopators—met its demise in the same manner as many other Highway 99 roadhouses. On the morning of May 20, 1935, a suspicious fire broke out, and the entire building was quickly engulfed in flames. Nearby residents described the blaze as "an inferno," and by the time the sun came up, all that remained was a smoldering pile of ashes. It was a dramatic ending to one of the most reviled of all local roadhouses.

MELBY'S ECHO LAKE TAVERN

It was way back in 1913 that Herman Butzke purchased a small chunk of land on Echo Lake, just off North Trunk Road, built a cabin and moved in with his wife and daughter. Butzke was famous in Seattle for being a singing bartender at one of the most infamous saloons in the city's history: the circa 1889 Billy Mug's Saloon (at 407½ Second Avenue). After North Trunk Road was paved and graded as part of the new highway project, a man by the name of Theodore Millan purchased a parcel of land from Butzke and constructed a roadside building in 1928. Millan reportedly used the triangular building to operate a roadhouse for the next few years, though its exact name (if any) remains unknown.

In 1933, when national liquor laws were relaxed and beer was allowed to be served again, a man by the name of Carl Melby purchased the building with the intent of turning it into a tavern. During Prohibition, Melby had been known as "Seattle's Society Bootlegger" after taking control of the city's liquor traffic following Roy Olmstead's incarceration at McNeil Island Penitentiary. A newspaper article at the time described Melby as being "the area's largest bonded liquor dealer in the northwest." He boasted quite the arrest record and was eventually sentenced to a prison work camp in 1931. The tavern was opened soon after his release and operated as Melby's Tavern for the next fifty years. Melby and his wife lived in the upstairs part of the building and ran the tavern down below. Throughout the 1930s and

'40s, Melby's Tavern was the site of several police visits for various liquor violations. This continued until Melby's death in 1942. Over the years, the tavern has managed to survive under various names and, as of this writing, is currently known as Woody's Tavern.

CHINALAND/CLUB CHARMLAND

It was around 1930 that Earl Coffrin founded an unusual "ride and dine" business on land at the northeast corner of 167th and Aurora Avenue. Patrons could select a horse from his stable, ramble along various dirt roads and trails throughout that neck of the woods, then enjoy a nice prepared meal. In 1935, Henry Kingzy Wong—who had previously run the Chinese Castle over on the Bothell Highway—bought the place and held the grand opening for his new Chinaland roadhouse (at 16708 Aurora Avenue) on September 12. Buss McClelland and His Musical Men, featuring "a sweet little girl, with a sweet, sweet voice," Lois Ray, along with the "internationally known" dance team of Lee & Roule, provided entertainment.

Above: Melby's Tavern, circa 1930s. *Courtesy Shoreline Historical Museum.*

Opposite, top: Club Charmland's formal "Grand Opening" display ad. *The* Seattle Times, *December 18, 1936.*

Opposite, bottom: Club Charmland, 1937. *Courtesy Puget Sound Regional Archives.*

GRAND OPENING
Saturday Night
Club Charmland

16708 AURORA AVE., SEATTLE

All New Band and Floor Show .. featuring

THE FIVE CHARMERS
NOVELTY SWING DANCE BAND

Greatest of All Masters of Ceremonies

SAM GORE
with an all-star Floor Show...all new acts...presenting

Phillips and Dolores	**Margaret Shearer**
Direct from Terrace Gardens, Chicago, in Novelty Dances new to the Northwest	*Real Singer of Real Songs*
Carol Oberg	**Dottie Dee**
The Snappy Tapper	*The Silver Venus*

NO COVER CHARGE AT THE CLUB CHARMLAND
MAKE NEW YEAR'S RESERVATIONS NOW
$3.00 PER PERSON   'PHONE RICHMOND 473

The Cosiest Chummy Spot on the Highway
ALWAYS A GOOD SHOW AND GOOD FOOD

In 1936, J. Woitt and Edna White acquired the venue, and their Club Charmland held its grand opening on the night of August 16, 1936, with "scintillating" dance music provided by Johnny Chitwood's orchestra. This new roadhouse clearly charmed one reporter, who deemed the dine-and-dance nightspot to be "the most attractive rendezvous in the Northwest." Woitt explained that the Charmland would be open nightly, excepting Mondays, and that dance music would initially be provided by Jack Wolcott's Orchestra, with floor show entertainments featuring Saint and Billy Corithers and Margie Douglas and Shirly Mills. In December, a second grand opening was promoted as featuring "a new band and floor show," along with the "Greatest of All Masters of Ceremonies," Sam Gore. This new musical ensemble was a novelty swing dance band, the Five Charmers. The "all-star Floor Show" acts included Phillips and Delores ("Direct from Terrace Gardens, Chicago, in Novelty Dances New to the Northwest"), Margaret Shearer ("Real Singer of Real Songs"), Carol "the Snappy Tapper" Oberg and Dottie "the Silver Venus" Dee. Although promoted as being "the Cosiest Chummy Spot on the Highway—Always a Good Show and Good Food," Club Charmland closed within the year.

COSTA'S CAFÉ

It was in 1945 that a noted chef from Seattle's Italian Club (at 620 Union Street), Costanzo "Costa" Lazzarotto—who had trained and worked in Italy, France, New York and Los Angeles—acquired the former Charmland building and opened his own dine-and-dance restaurant. "Chef Costa" was very well connected: he was personal friends with Governor Mon C. Wallgren and President Harry Truman, whom he once took out fishing. Then, after Washington's liquor laws were liberalized in November 1948, he attended a hearing of the King County Planning Commission on March 22, 1949, and submitted an application to run a legitimate cocktail bar. That's when one commissioner took a moment to tease him, bellowing: "I'm all for turning this application down flat! Any person who takes the *President of the United States* out salmon fishing in Puget Sound and catches only a *dogfish* should not receive any consideration from this board." After the laughter died down, Chef Costa got his liquor license. With cocktails now available, the restaurant was even more popular. Indeed, suburban legend holds that the likes of both Bob Hope and Frank Sinatra frequented the place when

Left: Chinaland's grand opening display ad. *The* Seattle Post-Intelligencer, *September 12, 1935.*

Right: Chef Costa held the grand opening of his café's new cocktail lounge in the former Club Charmland building on April 9, 1949. *The* Seattle Post-Intelligencer.

in town. Two decades later, the joint changed hands again, reemerging as Herb's Bavarian Inn, a nightclub that featured oompah music by Herb Mark's Bavarian Band. In 1973, the focus shifted to square dancing music, with a name change to the Barn, and the following year the business was recast as an old-timey roadhouse, the Drift On Inn. Later, the associated Club Hollywood Casino was built to the side, and gambling at its sixteen card tables commenced. Finally, though, after an electrical fire gutted the place, the club closed for good on April 11, 2015.

Chapter 7

OLD HIGHWAY 99 SOUTH

B ack in the 1880s, a few new travel routes began intersecting with the Military Road just south of Seattle. One that branched off was "Mike Kelly's Road," which later developed into the Des Moines Road. Decades went by, population density increased, automobiles came along and in July 1915, a new Seattle-Tacoma "scenic highway," the Highline Road (which was based in part on the old Des Moines Road and located a few miles to the west of the Pacific Highway), was opened to travelers. In time, scads of businesses and roadside attractions sprang up along these routes, and eventually locals would come to refer to the Pacific Highway as "Old Highway 99."

THE HALFWAY HOUSE

Owned by William A. Moody and his wife, Midge, the Halfway House (located "16 miles from Seattle—16 miles from Tacoma") was the "Home of Bill's Famous 10¢ Hamburger." In November 1931, they were fined by Justice of the Peace J.B. Wright "for permitting punchboards and slot machines to be operated" in their business. Punchboards were popular gambling devices that date to at least the late 1800s. A punchboard was a game of chance composed of a premade, commercially purchased wood or cardboard panel that had hundreds of holes. Each hole contained a rolled-up slip of paper and was covered with a foil or paper seal. Players paid the barkeep a fee, then used a metal stylus to punch open a hole and push a slip out of the back of the board. Each slip featured a number or combination of symbols corresponding to a chart that listed potential prizes ranging from cash to cigarettes to beer. No one got rich, no one got hurt and the bar made some money. Basically, it was just a low-key way to kill time.

Although seemingly a relatively harmless mode of gambling, punchboards were still illegal in some jurisdictions. Justice Wright wasn't quite finished: he also turned to the three of Sheriff Bannick's deputies who'd raided the joint and said: "It seems strange that you officers should have to go clear to Kent to find punchboards when there are thousands in operation between the courthouse and Pike Street." The concern was that some venues were paying the lawmen protection money and only those who weren't paying up were being popped. In 1937, Charles W. Banfield bought the place and managed it until 1951. By April 1952, the place was recast as Rusty's Halfway House, where one could enjoy a fried chicken dinner and relax to the organ music of Winifred Rhoades ("Star of Stage and Radio") in their Sea Shell Room. On July 18, 1958, a passing motorist noticed that the roof was aflame, and he stopped to warn about one hundred diners and the staff, who all fled safely.

THE BARN

With the recent liberalizing of various laws, scores of new joints opened, including the Barn, which was advertised as being "near the famous Halfway House." The Barn's grand opening on the night of September 16, 1933, promised attendees "FUN & FROLIC—Music and Dancing, Western Atmosphere, Kansas City Tommy Hayes and his entertainers—and the Prince of Beers: Alt Heidelberg Lager."

THE HI-LINE GROVE

The year 1940 brought another nightspot, the Grove, to this "Midway" stretch of the highway. Also advertised as being located at "Hi-Line, Next

Above: The Hi-Line Grove display ad, 1945. *The* Seattle Post-Intelligencer.

Left: The Hi-Line Grove display ad promoting setups of ice and cocktail mixers, plus dancing to the Toon-Toppers Orchestra. *The* Seattle Post-Intelligencer.

to the Halfway House," the Grove offered drivers "Dine—Dance—Chicken Dinner," plus live music by bands led by Don McConnell and, a bit later, by Joe Petsche.

THE BIG TREE INN (PART I)

This unique and eye-catching roadside attraction was built by carving out gigantic sections of a three-hundred-foot-tall, 2,500-year-old sequoia tree. It was originally constructed in 1915 for use as Humboldt County's exhibit at San Francisco's Panama Pacific International Exposition. The structure was later sold to a buyer who in 1921 had the two main sections—twenty feet and eighteen feet in diameter—shipped to the Seattle area, where it initially served as a home. Then in 1923, Andrew A. Swanson and his wife bought it and founded their Big Tree Inn resort ("Chicken dinners are a specialty") along "the High-Line Road" or "the old Seattle-Des Moines Highway." Their combination restaurant/gas station became a popular attraction, and local media often played it up. In a published guide to a scenic drive, the *Seattle Post-Intelligencer* noted that "interest is quickened by the Big Tree Inn, a complete inn-dwelling hollowed from the trunk of a gigantic redwood. With its rounded sides, heavy slab door, and tiny cut window panes it looks like a gnome's house."

The Big Tree Inn postcard, 1924. *Courtesy Northwest Music Archives.*

Business was good, but a few headaches still awaited the Swansons, like the government's announcement that it was rerouting the highway—news that meant the current volume of drivers passing by would be decreasing. Therefore, the Swansons decided that they needed to relocate. So, on August 9, 1938, they hired a moving company to hoist the Big Tree's sections and truck them a few miles eastward to a new spot along the Seattle-Tacoma Highway (at 19207 Pacific Highway South), where they began anew. Little could they have foreseen that the outbreak of World War II was on the horizon.

Chapter 8

THE END OF THE ROAD

Changes to American society and culture during and after the stressful World War II years were significant and widespread. Individuals as well as many businesses experienced painful challenges and suffering. As the *Seattle Post-Intelligencer* noted on December 6, 1942—just one day short of the first anniversary of the attack on Pearl Harbor—this season "finds the home front accepting new restrictions, curbs on normal living habits as the nation faces the second year of bitter warfare. Gasoline joined the growing list of rationed commodities last week.…Many articles are short stores this year, with others completely disappeared from stock. Gasoline rationing, which eliminates all unnecessary driving, throws a fatal punch at highway roadhouses, cafes and taverns. The *Post-Intelligencer* talked it over with proprietors of such highway landmarks as Big Tree Inn, Half-way House…and other spots on the Seattle-Tacoma Highway, and all indicated they're about to ready to throw in the towel. They're casualties of war on the home front."

THE BIG TREE INN (PART 2)

The Big Tree Inn was among the many roadside attractions that would suffer under the supply rationing during World War II. As Andrew Swanson would tell the *Seattle Post-Intelligencer* in November 1942: "First they moved the main highway from us, and we had to relocate here. And then came the Depression. And now comes shortages of all kinds." Even electricity was scarce, and "blackouts" were enforced over the government's fears that enemy airplanes could better locate targets if buildings and streets were lit. Blackouts, Swanson reported, "[make] it impossible for people to tell if we are open and operating at night, and next comes gas rationing." By the mid-1940s, E.R. Kennedy had bought the inn, but on May 23, 1947, a fire broke out in a storeroom, and although Kennedy fought it valiantly with a garden hose, the big tree went up in flames.

Scoop Jackson vs. the Roadhouses

Throughout the 1930s and '40s, several other roadhouses emerged along the new Everett Highway, though most lasted only a very short time. They included such notable places as Dutcher's—a local roadside attraction known by locals as the "Windmill" due to the large rotating windmill that was attached to the front of the building. The interior of Dutcher's featured two dance floors and four bars, which quickly earned the place some notoriety. Other Highway 99 roadhouses included the Golden Slipper, the Lido, Merry Max and Dine, Willows Tavern, Valentine's Suburban Cafe, the Brookside Inn and Albright's Bungalow Cafe, which operated at the site of what is now Harvey's Tavern.

By the late 1930s, as local residents became more and more fed up with the lawlessness surrounding the inns and roadhouses along the Everett Highway, an up-and-coming young attorney by the name of Henry Martin Jackson was elected as prosecuting attorney for Snohomish County. More commonly known by his nickname, "Scoop" Jackson, the young crime fighter had vowed to clean up the liquor, prostitution and gambling that

Opposite: Dutcher's Roadhouse matchbook, circa 1930s. *Brad Holden's collection*.

Above: The *Seattle Times* hails Congressman Henry M. Jackson's war against criminals and their gambling dens on October 10, 1948.

LOST ROADHOUSES OF SEATTLE

had plagued the area for over a decade. Jackson wasted no time in cracking down on the roadhouses, personally leading the sheriff and his deputies on weekly raids and making sure that all arrests led to successful prosecutions. By 1940, he had made quite a name for himself by putting several well-known bootleggers and corrupt club owners behind bars, as well as cleaning up any establishments that offered gambling. At that time, slot machines and pinball machines had become quite problematic along the south end of Highway 99, so Jackson made it a point to snuff out gambling. This earned Jackson a certain degree of legal fame, which he used to launch a successful political career serving the state of Washington as both a U.S. representative and, later, as a U.S. senator. The effects of Jackson's war against the roadhouses were felt quickly, and by the time he assumed political office, several of the illegal clubs along Highway 99 had been forced to close down. In this sense, his term as the local prosecutor served as a symbolic end to the golden era of Highway 99 roadhouses. Those that survived the Jackson years, such as the Ranch, typically rebranded themselves as a more legitimate form of nightclub or cabaret, though they still tended to operate within a legal gray area.

It was on January 4, 1954, that the City of Seattle took steps to annex a ten-square-mile area from North 85th Street to North 145th Street (and between Puget Sound and Lake Washington), shifting the city limits boundary northwards and finally placing much of both the old Bothell Road/Victory Way/Bothell Highway and the Pacific Highway/State Route 99/Aurora Avenue North roadhouse strips under city control. That action signaled the end of an era, and in short order, nearly all the local roadhouses had disappeared off the map.

Chapter 9

THE ROADHOUSE LEGACY

Back during in the roadhouse heyday, the highways and byways all across Washington were lined with many more dine-and-dance and BYOB joints than could ever be covered in one book. But let's go ahead and give a nod to some of them. Back in the day, it seems practically every rural lake or beach in western Washington boasted a dance pavilion, such as those built at Angle Lake, Diamond Lake, Echo Lake, Haller Lake, Henderson Lake, Lake Geneva, Lake Killarney, Lake Stevens, North Lake, Patterson Lake, Richmond Beach, Star Lake and Steel Lake.

Lake Washington alone had dance pavilions at Madison Park, Leschi Park, Juanita Park, the Lonesome Park at Lake Washington on the Renton Highway and the Rainier Boulevard Park, with dancing on Saturdays to Ed Long's Dance Orchestra and Warren Anderson's Popular Orchestra. Among the "resorts" that offered dancing were Alder Beach Manor at Des Moines ("Dancing every evening"), Sutherland's Resort on Five Mile Lake, Nolt's Dancing Pavilion at American Lake and Vasa Park at Lake Sammamish, Foss' Shadow Lake Ballroom, Gaffney's Grove at Lake Wilderness and another at Trout Lake, which was based in a log cabin and later became Mickey's Chicken Dinner restaurant. Then there was Ovington's Summer Resort (at Lake Crescent, with "electric light…our own garden…boating… dancing") and Gustav Bresemann's Dance Hall at Lake Spanaway, which had a reputation for wildness, such that when it began hosting dance marathons—which, according to writer Nancy Covert, "were considered immoral and exploitive"—it was raided by the law and shut down.

SOUTHERN FRIED
CHICKEN
& STEAKS
Served in the "Glorified"
Manor
THE BEST IN
DINING
& DANCING
Dinners from 6 P. M.
Dancing from 9:30 P. M.

The MANOR
(Formerly THE PLANTATION)
BOTHELL WAY at 145
for Reservations Call SH.9222

The Manor, "formerly the Plantation," display ad promoting "southern fried" dinners and dancing. *The* Seattle Times, *undated clipping.*

Some of the other popular nightspots included the Palladium Ballroom (at 125th and the Seattle-Everett Hi-Way); the 7 Gables Inn, with its rooster signage (at 20842 Pacific Highway South, fifteen miles south of Seattle); Club Moderne (formerly Max Frolic's Villa, two miles south of Tacoma on the "Olympia Hi-Way"); Century Ballroom (at 1406 54th Avenue East, in Fife); Beacon Ballroom (at Birch Bay); McDonald's Grove (eight miles south of Renton on the Maple Valley Highway); Belfair Barn (on the old Belfair Highway), which was torched by the local fire department as a training exercise in 1987; and several more that eventually caught fire accidentally or via arson, including the circa 1924 Firwood Roadhouse (at Fife), which burned in 2008; the Holiday Ballroom (at Burlington), which burned in the 1960s; the Seven Cedars Ballroom (at Mount Vernon), which burned in 1963; the Playquato Ballroom (at Chehalis), which burned in 1975; the circa 1927 Tropics Ballroom (seven miles west of Olympia, at Schneider's Prairie on Old Highway 101), which the Nisqually earthquake of 2001 destroyed, and whose remains burned in 2008; and Perl Maurer's circa 1934 Perl's Dance Pavilion (at 3536 Arsenal Way, Bremerton), which was torched by an arsonist in 1959, was rebuilt by 1961 and burned again in 2018.

The vast majority of the Evergreen State's old roadhouses have for varying reasons—legal abatements, changing times, property sales and accidental or arson fires—slipped away and are long gone. Among the exceedingly few that for decades remained true to their original purpose—to provide a comfortable gathering place to eat, drink, mix, mingle and dance—were the following few venues: the Evergreen Ballroom (along the "old Olympia-Tacoma Highway"), the Spanish Castle Ballroom (midway on the "new Seattle-Tacoma Highway"), Parker's Ballroom (on the "old Seattle-Everett Highway"), the Jolly Roger Roadhouse and Mack's Shanty (both on the Bothell Highway), Fiddler's Inn

The Rainier Boulevard Park Dance Pavilion grand opening display ad. *The* Seattle Times, *March 30, 1921.*

(off the beaten path, over on Thirty-Fifth Avenue Northeast) and the Wagon Wheel Inn (at Federal Way, along the old "Pacific Highway South")—most of which originally opened for business during the challenging days of Prohibition. Of those, only the latter three remain extant.

THE EVERGREEN BALLROOM

It was back in 1931 that a musician named Walter Sholund built and opened the Evergreen Ballroom—a classic barn-style venue built from old-growth timbers—on the northern outskirts of the capital city of Olympia (at today's

9121 Pacific Avenue Southeast). Sholund also led the house band, and his hall became established as a favorite local dining and dancing spot for Olympians, as well as Tacomans who were willing to travel twenty miles south—indeed, the place became a destination magnet for entertainment-starved people from miles around.

In addition to booking various territory bands to play old-time country hoedowns, the hall also occasionally brought in a dance orchestra from Seattle or Tacoma to try to attract the collegiate foxtrot or jitterbug set. But as the tough economic times of the Great Depression took hold, the Sholunds sought ways to increase business. One breakthrough was their realization that a whole segment of the local population wasn't necessarily being served: the countless African American servicemen at the nearby Fort Lewis army base. Sholund began diversifying the talent he booked. Some members of the community didn't appreciate this change, and Sholund got an earful about the matter from a few rednecks. So when his ballroom mysteriously caught fire and burned to the ground in 1932, rumors circulated that it had fallen victim to arson by local racists.

But Sholund stepped up and immediately began rebuilding, this time with a larger, 1,670-square-foot maple dance floor, and the "Green"—as locals came to fondly call it—came to life once again. Although there is no evidence that the Evergreen ever provided illicit alcohol to its patrons, a longstanding tradition arose of patrons holding alcohol-fueled pre-functions in their cars out in the parking lot. That area itself earned a reputation as a place for rumbles—as the *Daily Olympian* later noted, "Old-timers around the county remember The Green as a knock-down-and-drag-out, foot-stomping, two-by-four bustout joint where fists could fly at the drop of an insult."

Sipping from a pocket flask and getting into some friendly Friday night fisticuffs aside, it was really the music that drew crowds here, and the place became a legendary tour stop for a few decades' worth of America's top musical performers. The venerable dance hall brought in the best big bands of the 1930s and '40s, the country music stars of the '40s and '50s and some of the earliest local shows by the first generation of '50s rock 'n' rollers. Among the unforgettable headliners were such marquee attractions as the dance orchestras led by Louis Armstrong, Duke Ellington, Count Basie, Benny Goodman, Harry James, Lionel Hampton, Tommy Dorsey and Woody Herman. A few of the country legends who graced its stage were Roy Acuff, Hank Williams, T. Texas Tyler, Ray Price, Hank Thompson, Ferlin Husky, Marty Robbins, Faron Young and Johnny Cash. Jazz stars included Charlie "Bird" Parker, Dinah Washington, Nat King

The Evergreen Ballroom, 1940. *Courtesy Thurston County Assessor, Washington State Archives.*

Cole, Dave Brubeck and Chet Baker. Along the way, the ballroom also served as a nurturing incubator for local stars such as Seattle's Ray Charles and Bonnie Guitar and Tacoma's Buck Owens.

The rock 'n' roll era began here in 1956 with a show by Bill Haley and His Comets, and others followed, including Fats Domino, Little Richard, Chuck Berry, Gene Vincent and Jerry Lee Lewis. Many top R&B acts also graced the stage here, including B.B. King, Bill Doggett, Roy Brown, Earl Bostic, Jimmy Reed, James Brown and his Famous Flames, Etta James, Hank Ballard and the Midnighters, Little Willie John, Ike & Tina Turner, Jackie Wilson, Bobby "Blue" Bland, "Little Junior" Parker, the Drifters, the Platters, the Coasters and Marvin Gaye. One particularly notable night came in September 1957 when a Los Angeles–based singer, Richard Berry, brought his song "Louie" north; it ended up becoming the Northwest's signature rock song after being covered by Tacoma's pioneering rock band, the Wailers, and then by Portland's Kingsmen and Paul Revere & the Raiders. All three of those hitmakers—as well as other top Northwest teen bands including the Dave Lewis Combo, Merrilee Rush and the Turnabouts, Don and the Goodtimes, the Sonics, the Bards and many more—all relished their opportunities to gig the Green.

The Evergreen Ballroom undated display ad promoting Irv Sholund's dance band. *Courtesy Northwest Music Archives.*

In 1967, when Interstate 5 was finally completed, the north–south traffic flow was generally improved, but that change also unfortunately steered the vast majority of travelers (and touring musicians) away from the old Highway 99 route. The Green was now off the beaten path, and its fate was sealed. A series of new owners tried to hang on, weathering waves of musical revolutions ranging from psychedelic acid rock, to country rock, to heavy metal, to hip hop. In 1983, one owner tried unsuccessfully to recast it as a topless bar, and along the way, the old dance floor began to surrender turf to an increasingly popular billiard zone. Finally, it was announced that the Green would reemerge as a gambling casino, but on July 20, 2000, a fire broke out in the Green's kitchen, and the beloved hall's dancing days were finally done.

Spanish Castle Ballroom

When constructed in 1931 by its founders, Archie Bacon and Frank Enos, this hall was purposefully situated at Midway, an area located literally midway between Seattle and Tacoma that was also sometimes referred to as the "Hi-Line." That site—just outside of the city limits on unincorporated county land—was selected specifically in order to escape those towns' ongoing efforts to clamp down on nightlife activities. The Spanish Castle's grand opening event nevertheless drew huge crowds from both distant towns, who were likely attracted by the big band sounds of the Frankie Roth Orchestra and the promise of a great new recessed dance floor. Then there was the spectacle of the new building itself (located near the corner of old Highway 99, now Pacific Highway South, and the Kent Des Moines Road). The ballroom was designed to look like a storybook caricature of an ancient Moorish fortress. Its exotic architectural details—including a stucco structure with neon accents—successfully evoked mystery and romance and instantly became a roadside attraction in and of themselves. With Prohibition's repeal, the Castle began selling beer in 1934; prior to that, patrons had partied in their cars outside and often slipped in carrying pocket flasks for ongoing social lubrication. In 1937, the Castle was sold off to a new partnership consisting of M.W. "Wes" Morrill (founder of First Bank in Kent, Washington) and C.L. Knutsen (a local auto dealer).

But one thing that remained constant throughout those years was the house band. Roth led his orchestra in weekly shows up through 1942, when he stepped aside and his trombonist, Gordon Greene, took over. Those World War II years proved to be the peak for the Castle—a time when as many as two thousand folks attended dances that were necessarily scheduled in shifts to correspond with the labor shifts in war industry factories. Those big band swing dances continued regularly up until 1962, but by 1959, their popularity had declined to the point that they were limited to just Saturday nights. Fridays suddenly opened up, and thus in October 1959, an enterprising local radio DJ, Pat O'Day, booked the area's most prominent band, the Wailers, to play what would be the very first of countless rock 'n' roll teen dances held at the Castle. And so began the area's golden era of teen dances—as well as a tradition of beer-powered parking lot rumbles. At the turn of the decade, various DJs began bringing touring rock 'n' roll stars to the Castle, including Gene Vincent, Jerry Lee Lewis, Roy Orbison and Johnny Burnette. Other shows featured pop stars (Tony Orlando, Freddie Cannon, Ray Stevens, Johnny

Rivers, Bobby Vee, Jan & Dean and Herb Alpert & the Tijuana Brass) as well as country acts like Ernest Tubb and Conway Twitty. Along the way, plenty of local teen bands got their chance to play the Castle, including the Adventurers, Amazing Aztecs, Casuals, Checkmates, Cut-Ups, Dynamics, Frantics, Playboys, Sonics, Statics and the Swags.

A guitarist with the Checkers (and future jazz star) Larry Coryell recalled those days: "I remember gigs at the Spanish Castle with the Checkers backing up Ray Stevens—and another time when we backed up Gene Vincent. It was the *thrill* of our *life* to play the Spanish Castle!" In 1961, the Wailers recorded their best-selling *At the Castle* album in the hall, and one of their biggest fans was a teenage guitarist named Jimmy Hendrix. Many years after Hendrix had altered his name to Jimi and become an international rock star, his father, Al, would recall that his son would "go to the clubs and ask the guy could he sit in with him. He used to do that right here in Seattle when he was coming up. He used to go to the place on Old 99, the dancehall, the Spanish Castle. He used to go there and hang around the stage and try to get in and play with some of the groups." Hendrix's lingering fondness for Seattle's music scene is indicated by the fact that years after he left the Northwest, he penned "Spanish Castle Magic" in tribute to his days hanging out at the old roadhouse. Dave Marsh probably put it best in his book *Louie Louie: The History and Mythology of the World's Most Famous Rock 'n' Roll Song*:

> *Once you know the legend of the Wailers at the Castle and the facts of Jimi's attendance there, the lyrics of his "Spanish Castle Magic" seem haunted by homesick nostalgia. "It's very far away, it takes about half a day / To get there by my ah…dragonfly," he sings, in the voice of a kid stranded a couple continents from home.*

Later in the tune, Hendrix offers one last global-positioning clue for the literal-minded: "No it's not in Spain."

In the summer of 1963, Ian Whitcomb—then a British student out touring the States (and just a bit prior to launching his own pop music career)—happened through Seattle, and he recalled in his *Rock Odyssey* book that it was at the Castle that he was first exposed to our regional rock traditions: "I journeyed out with a beer-bellied kid to a dance hall called the Spanish Castle to hear some of the instrumental groups who specialized in the Northwest sound. I was lucky enough that night to hear the Kingsmen play their current hit, 'Louie Louie.' They wore band jackets and looked fairly clean cut, but when they blasted out on this number the kids went wild."

The Spanish Castle Ballroom, viewed from the north, March 4, 1940. *Courtesy Ron Edge.*

The Spanish Castle Ballroom, viewed from the east, circa 1940. *Courtesy of the Greater Des Moines/Zenith Historical Society.*

Such teen dances—not to mention the many high school proms, parking lot rumbles and amorous backseat rendezvous that also occurred at the Spanish Castle—were definite highlights for a generation or two of local youth. But the Spanish Castle's days were, unfortunately, numbered. Two separate incidents where teenagers were run down in the roadway out front dimmed the Castle's magic, Pat O'Day chose to quit booking shows there and the historic structure was finally razed by bulldozers in April 1968.

Parker's Dance Pavilion

In 1929, Dick Parker—the owner of his namesake Parker's Highway Pavilion over on the Bothell Highway—built a second, bigger and better dance hall, this one along the "New Seattle-Everett Highway" (today's Aurora Avenue North). Its location, like that of so many other roadhouses, was purposefully selected, as it was just outside of Seattle's northern city limits (then drawn at 85th Street). Parker acquired a five-acre plot at 170th Street, and construction got underway in 1929. Parker's self-built hall was a remarkable architectural marvel; the thing was basically a twenty-thousand-square-foot, wide-open dance floor with absolutely no posts obstructing views. Parker hired an accomplished local builder named Dave Markley to construct the springy dance floor itself, telling Markley he wanted one that would "bounce."

When Parker's Dance Pavilion opened for business in 1930, Parker kicked off a long streak of booking popular local acts (including Put Anderson and his Dixieland Band and orchestras led by Frankie Roth, Burke Garrett and Max Pillar), as well as a number of national touring stars, such as the dance orchestras led by Tommy Dorsey, Guy Lombardo and Jan Garber. But with Prohibition still in effect and the Great Depression dragging the economy down, times were so tough that by 1932 Parker had resorted to advertising his dance hall as "Dick Parker's Roller Rink" in order to attract a different clientele: skaters. For years after Prohibition ended in 1934, the ballroom existed as "bottle club," where customers brought in their own booze (kept in a brown paper bag under their table), and the house sold them setups. As a result, Parker's was among the many local rooms that were now finally free to sell beer and/or other alcoholic beverages.

Without seeking to cast any aspersions on Dick Parker—or to engage in guilt by association—it is interesting to note that on November 4, 1936, his brother Harold was "arrested by alcohol tax unit agents in connection with the

GORDON GREENE'S SPANISH CASTLE ORCHESTRA

Top: Gordon Greene's Spanish Castle Orchestra postcard, 1950s. *Courtesy Northwest Music Archives.*

Bottom: Dick Parker's Pavilion, 1937. *Courtesy Washington State Archives.*

seizure of a 500-gallon still" and was "bound over to the federal grand jury." Charged with infractions of "revenue laws"—the "possession of untaxed liquor"—he was convicted and sentenced to a one-hundred-dollar fine and fifteen months' hard time at Washington's McNeil Island Penitentiary.

Dick Parker died in 1940, and his second wife, Dodie, followed shortly after. Ownership of the business passed to her sisters, Kelma Shoemaker and Opel Horn, and later to Shoemaker's sons, Vern and Darrell Amundson, and

Dick Parker's Pavilion display ad promoting Frankie Roth and his Sophisticated Rhythm Boys, 1948. *The* Seattle Times.

Opal's son, Skip Horn. In the late 1950s, the management finally rebelled against local Musicians Union–enforced restrictions and began booking Black musicians into "Parker's Ballroom"—in particular two popular R&B bands, Billy Tolles and his Vibrators and the Dave Lewis Combo. Then the first wave of rock 'n' roll stars began coming through town, and management booked shows by such icons as Jerry Lee Lewis, Gene Vincent and Bobby Darin. Later years saw other stars coming through, including the Beach Boys, Them (with Van Morrison), Sam the Sham and Buffalo Springfield.

Meanwhile, numerous other young local combos scored gigs here, including Clayton Watson and his Silhouettes, the Fleetwoods, Frantics, Little Bill and the Bluenotes, Tiny Tony and the Statics, Wailers, Viceroys, Paul Revere & the Raiders, Kingsmen, Merrilee and the Turnabouts and the Sonics. In 1964, the Dynamics released their classic *Dynamics at Parker's* album, and the Ballroom became solidified as the center of the north end's teen dance action. The last local rock band to play Parker's was White Heart—the precursor to the mega-successful Northwest '70s band Heart. The last ever dance at Parker's featured Max Pillar's big band—an ensemble that had played there regularly since the 1950s. Years later, the *Seattle Times* quoted Pillar casting his memory back to that closing night: "It was the last of the big ballrooms to close its doors—truly the end of an era. Most of us wondered, 'where do we go from here?'" Alas, there was no easy or satisfying answer for him and his generation.

Parker's did, however, successfully weather those changing times—but only by going through radical updates. In 1970, it was recast as the hippie-dippie Aquarius Tavern. And although its first scheduled dance in this new incarnation was a flop—the Buddy Miles Express was a no-show—the place succeeded very well over the years, bringing in acts that ranged from A to Z, including Aerosmith, America, BTO, Badfinger, the Byrds, Albert Collins, the Guess Who, Albert King, the Ohio Players, Johnnie Otis, the Righteous Brothers, Al Stewart, George Strait, Muddy Waters, Koko Taylor, Toots and the Maytals, the Ventures and Warren Zevon.

In addition, whole new generations of local bands—including Acapulco Gold, Annie Rose & the Thrillers, Bighorn, Burgundy Express, Child, Epicentre, Gabriel, Jr. Cadillac, Kidd Afrika and Heart—developed sizeable fan bases in part because of their Aquarius appearances. In fact, one of Heart's shows there in 1975 was captured live on tape, and a few years later (after they'd broken out as an international hit act), those recordings were issued on their *Magazine* LP.

By 1980, the hall required some spiffing up, and the owners committed themselves to a $1 million remodel in an effort to revamp it as a full-blown "supper club." With an all-new commercial kitchen, the renamed Parker's Restaurant also continued to bring in touring stars like Elvin Bishop, Blue Öyster Cult, Ray Charles, Joe Cocker, Crowded House, Joan Jett, B.B. King, Marshall Tucker, John Mayall, Simply Red and Tina Turner. In October 1993, a three-day weekend spree of rock dances featuring Paul Revere & the Raiders marked the final days of Parker's Ballroom. After that, the place was recast once again—this time as a gambling joint called Parker's Sports Bar & Casino. In April 2012, the place—true to form for a roadhouse—received legal notice to cease its gambling operations: "According to charging documents, the owner and holder of the gaming licenses had sold his interest in Parker's to a new owner without notifying the state and without the new owner applying for licenses under his own name….There was also reference to back taxes." Oops. By the following November, Parker's had finally cashed in its chips, and demolition of the once-proud old ballroom began. Today, the historic site is home to a common car lot.

Bert Lindgren's Bothell Hi-Way Pavilion

It was back in 1935 that Dick Parker sold his Highway Pavilion on the Bothell Highway to musician/businessman Bert Lindgren. For the first few years, Lindgren kept the business's name and worked to build up a clientele that would be attracted to his Old-Time Band's offering of Scandinavian schottisches, polkas and other traditional song forms. In 1938, Lindgren renamed it the Bothell Hi-Way Pavilion, and for decades, he, an accomplished accordionist, led the Old-Time Band (with featured vocalist Laurene Lindgren). The hall's dance floor remained packed right up until 1956, when the music ended after a fire torched the place.

The Washington Social and Educational Club

For many years after Prohibition's repeal, there existed remnants of the old battles, which were kept alive due to a tangle of laws on the books—plus various unofficial policies—that worked in tandem to keep a lid on the action. But this situation also perpetuated a dysfunctional and corrupt political and business culture that saw the ongoing sale and/or serving of illegal, untaxed, smuggled liquor. Indeed, three-and-a-half decades after the repeal of Prohibition, easily one hundred taverns, bars, restaurants and clubs in Seattle were still operating outside the strict rules of the law. The story of one of those—the Washington Social and Educational Club (WSEC)—is emblematic of the whole era.

Back in the day, it was an unofficial City of Seattle policy to limit the establishment of commercial nightlife venues within the largely Black neighborhoods of the Central District (CD). But then, on February 19, 1946, the *Seattle Times* reported this welcome bit of news: "An unwritten but rigid policy of the city council, forbidding cabarets east of Eighth Avenue in the central portion of the city, was relaxed yesterday, to give Seattle's Negro community a dine-and-dance establishment at the Savoy Ballroom, 2203 E. Madison St., operators of which were granted a cafe-dance license." But even prior to that breakthrough, one particular local Black businessman, Sirless "Sy" Groves, had seemingly found a way to finesse the rules that limited where, when and how alcoholic beverages could be served to the public.

Sy Groves had cleverly incorporated his business—the Washington Social and Educational Club (at 2302 East Madison Street, or 104½ Twenty-

GRAND OPENING SATURDAY NIGHT
SEPTEMBER 10TH
BOTHELL HI-WAY PAVILION
BERT LINDGREN'S
(ACCORDIONIST)
OLD TIME BAND
DANCING SATURDAYS 9 TILL 2

The Bothell Hi-Way Pavilion's grand opening display ad. *The* Seattle Post-Intelligencer, *September 9, 1938.*

Third Avenue North)—in 1944 as a "private" members-only organization. You know, just like those whites-dominated, and legally favored, Moose and Elk clubs! And so, for a while, good times could be had there; patrons danced to the music of touring jazz and R&B stars, including Cab Calloway, Charlie "Bird" Parker, Lester Young, Dexter Gordon, T-Bone Walker, Jack McVea and B.B. King. Local talents also performed here, including Bumps Blackwell's bands—which at times featured future stars such as Ray Charles, Ernestine Anderson and Quincy Jones. The latter's recollection of those days in his autobiography were vivid: "I never did figure out where the Reverend Groves' church was, nor did I know how his club got the 'education' part of that title, unless you consider the act of lifting a peach jar full of VAT 69 whiskey to your lips and sliding it down your throat educational, but the Reverend's club was definitely social. People brought bottles of whiskey and wine in paper bags, paid a dollar or two for a 'setup' from the club—a bucket of ice, four water glasses, and maybe some soda pop—and then partied all night long drinking whiskey and eating home-cooked barbeque while watching us play." It was a room players loved to play and where partiers loved to party. The popular—and sometimes way over legal capacity—venue would see many a wild night and more than one news-making police raid: "Occasionally there were police busts, fistfights, even gunfire," Jones continued, "and we'd have to haul ass out the back door."

By 1947, the powers that be had finally had enough, and the Seattle Police Department began a crackdown on numerous after-hours venues. That year alone, they raided ninety-some nightclubs that were noncompliant with liquor laws that still—a quarter of a century after the repeal of Prohibition—forbade the sale of cocktails. And thus, on October 8, 1948, the authorities raided the WSEC, nabbing 166 people in what jazz historian Paul de Barros described as "the largest arrest ever made in a Seattle speakeasy." The accused were marched out to East Madison and hauled away in numerous paddy wagons. A mere month later, Washington State's liquor laws were finally liberalized to allow the sale of cocktails, yet the WSEC remained under continual threat of police raids. According to Caitlin Cleary, Paul de Barros and Melanie McFarland, this was "in part because of attempts to shift profits from newly legalized alcohol by the drink from black neighborhoods to downtown clubs."

Thus it was that in July 1950, Groves himself was arrested after officers claimed they saw five sailors in possession of liquor bottles in the club late on a Saturday night—violating a city liquor ordinance that "prohibits drinking in clubs between midnight Saturday and 6 o'clock Monday morning." Though Groves was tried and found guilty, a jury later overturned the conviction based on the fact that nobody testified to witnessing the sailors actually drinking. That same year brought blaring newspaper headlines playing up a story about an off-duty policeman who was stabbed while working as a bouncer at the WSEC. Then, with the law and the media dogging the WSEC, Groves's troubles increased when he was arrested again on October 30, 1950—this time after two plainclothes cops were served fifty-cent glasses of low-alcohol "near beer." The duo had each also bought "membership" tickets, yet Groves was cited for running a cabaret rather than a private club, though a judge found him innocent of the charge in January 1951. By that late date, the WSEC had been formally abated, and it was finally shuttered that year. As of 2022, the WSEC building still stands.

THE CHINA PHEASANT

It was on August 27, 1940, that Danny Woo and Kai Eng opened their China Pheasant restaurant at 10315 East Marginal Way (one mile south of Boeing Field on a stretch of the old Seattle-Tacoma Highway). In addition to a full dining menu, the place also offered ample amounts of drinking, dancing and gambling and soon established itself as "a real swinging roadhouse." The ornately decorated nightclub boasted a large dance floor surrounded by glowing Chinese lanterns and quickly became known for its live music; local acts such as Abe Brashen and his Orchestra would perform every night to a packed house. The Bob Harvey Orchestra performed there regularly throughout the 1940s, with one newspaper describing the place

Left: The China Pheasant souvenir photograph folder, undated. *Courtesy Northwest Music Archives.*

Below: Bob Harvey's dance band onstage at the China Pheasant, 1940s. *Courtesy Northwest Music Archives.*

as "the area's most colorful gambling and night spot." In 1944, Seattle's first traditional New Orleans–style Dixieland jazz band—as led by the noted pianist Johnny Wittwer—drew throngs to the China Pheasant.

Within a couple years of opening, the establishment fell under the ownership of Harry Lew, who added even more gambling. This quickly caught the attention of local authorities, leading to the China Pheasant's first raid in 1942. King County deputies burst through the front doors on a Saturday afternoon and arrested the club's lone occupant—a Chinese chef who happened to have some gambling paraphernalia near him in the kitchen while he was preparing food. This would be the first of many such police raids due to various gambling violations. During a raid in 1945, Lew was promptly arrested after police discovered a large amount of gambling equipment. As a result, he would serve two years at Walla Walla State Penitentiary.

The China Pheasant was eventually sold to a Black entrepreneur named Wilmer Morgan, who also operated the Mardi Gras Grill and the Birdland dance hall in the Central District. Despite the change in ownership, the nightclub continued to run afoul of the law well into the 1950s and '60s. In April 1962, agents from the WSLCB raided the joint after somebody snitched on an illegal after-hours party. After this final raid, the China Pheasant was shut down for good, and the building was then used as an auction house. On September 1, 1965, the building was completely destroyed after a mysterious fire broke out. The exact cause of the fire was never determined.

THE JOLLY ROGER (PART 2)

By the late 1970s, this old roadhouse (at 8720 Lake City Way) had transformed into a popular blues joint—one that Tacoma's future guitar star Robert Cray used as an early outpost. In 1979, community preservationists successfully petitioned to have this prime example of 1930s roadside vernacular

The Jolly Roger, 1976. Photograph by John Margolies. *Courtesy Library of Congress, Prints & Photographs Division, LC-DIG-mrg-07228.*

Jolly Roger Roadhouse display ad (replete with counterfactual startup date) promoting album release party for Seattle's premiere bluesman Isaac Scott and his band. *The Seattle Times.*

architecture listed as an official City of Seattle landmark. Then, from 1980 into 1982, it was recast by chef Mauriceau Castro as the Jolly Roger Roma, an Italian restaurant—but one where the blues still ruled. In February 1984, four of the Northwest's premier groups—the Paul DeLay Band, the Tom McFarland Blues Band, Curtis Salgado & In Yo' Face and the Isaac Scott band—were recorded live, resulting in the 1985 album *Live at the Roadhouse.* In time, the joint went full circle back to being a Chinese restaurant, the Hunan Wok, which struggled along until reportedly succumbing to arson on October 19, 1989. After the building's remains were finally demolished in March 1991, a banal Shell Oil service station was erected on the site.

The Wagon Wheel Inn/Brooklake Inn

Constructed in 1929, out in the wilds just off Pacific Highway South near today's town of Federal Way, a twenty-acre roadhouse/dance hall called the Wagon Wheel Inn offered patrons all the fun they could stand. Nearby illegal still operations provided the speakeasy its moonshine, while the multiple cribs upstairs served as an on-site brothel. In addition, a gambling den run by the manager, R.K. "Ricky" Ruffo, was situated in the basement. The large barnlike building attracted a loyal clientele, plenty of whom were rough types. Indeed, the admission window near the north entrance near the parking lot was "where patrons were asked to check their brass knuckles, knives and guns." Even after defying Prohibition laws up through their repeal in 1933, the Inn stubbornly carried on its nefarious activities. By 1935, it had been recast as Rickey's Club, and the vice continued until the King County sheriff had finally had enough.

A prosecuting attorney's filing for a restraining order read, in part:

> *For a long time past* [Rickey's] *constituted and now constitutes a house and place where gambling is carried on or permitted, and is a house or place on a public road where drunkenness, gambling, fighting, or breaches of the peace are carried on or permitted with the knowledge of the…owners and others.*

A court order followed, pegging the joint as an "attractive nuisance"; then, after being shuttered for five peaceful years, in 1943 the property was converted into the Brooklake Club House, which still stands (at 726 South 356th Street Federal Way) and is now operated by a consortium of local civic clubs. In more recent times, the Brooklake Hall served as a rental space where bikers and hot rod clubs held their shindigs.

The Brooklake Inn parking lot and entry, undated. *Courtesy Historical Society of Federal Way.*

The Brooklake Inn lakeside view, undated. *Courtesy Historical Society of Federal Way.*

In addition, independently produced rock shows—er, keggers—kept the tradition of illicit alcohol consumption alive. The 1980s and '90s brought heavy metal to the hall via bands like Alice in Chains, Bloodgood, Bolt Thrower, Cold Steele, Jagged Dagger, Paladin, Phoenix and Whiskey Fix. Notably, a gig by one of the area's top '80s metal bands, Forced Entry, was interrupted by a police raid and shut down. It seems that some things never change. And along the way, scads of punks, grungers and alt rockers all came through as well: Ambush, Aspirin Feast, Basket Case, Biohazard, Blue Collar, Bone Cellar, Confused, Conifer Bog, Daft, Dandilyon Soup, Dead Precious, Death of Earth, Dekay, Delilah, Dirty Cartoons, Disallegiance, Dumpt, Exploited, Fall-Outs, Flathead, Gas Huffer, Girl Trouble, Gorles, Hangnail, Insubordinate Youth, Leaky Green, Menaces, Mr. Yuk, Never Forever, nubbin, Oxygen Freak, Pestilence, Platonic Bondage, Purdins, Rat City, Rhino Humpers, Sedated Souls, Seditionaries, Sleep Capsule, Type O Negative, UKC3, Unearth, Versatellers, Violaters, Warfrats and Weathervane.

FIDDLER'S INN

Walter R. Haines built his rustic log cabin–style roadhouse way out in the wilds of Seattle's Wedgwood neighborhood in 1934. He was a South Dakota farm boy who as a teen had hopped a freight train heading out west, arriving in Seattle in 1922. Musically inclined—he played the spoons, the cornet and eventually the tuba and the bull fiddle—Haines initially scored a gig playing with the orchestra at the grand Olympic Hotel (at 411 University Street) and later gigged with Seattle's most prominent dance band as led by Vic Meyers. By 1934, he was leading the Walt Haines Orchestra—performing live on KXA radio in a timeslot shared with Perl Maurer's Orchestra, whose home base was the Perl's Dance Pavilion roadhouse over in Bremerton.

The Great Depression was tough on all the arts, and soon after the repeal of Prohibition, Haines took up a new line of work: opening his own tavern, the Fiddler's Inn. He wisely selected a corner lot (at today's 9219 Thirty-Fifth Avenue Northeast) that was conveniently situated across the road from a gas station. The Inn became a popular roadhouse, and Haines was known for entertaining patrons by playing the spoons, as well as leading several bands to the Inn over the decades. Among the notable musicians who performed at the Inn back in the 1930s was Paul Tutmarc, a local radio singer, music teacher, guitarist, inventor and leader of a series of string bands. Tutmarc is best remembered these days for having designed and marketed the world's first "electric bass fiddle" (e.g., bass guitar) under his Audiovox brand.

In 1948, the Inn got busted for selling beer to minors and had its license briefly suspended. In 1949—when Jay T. MacVair was managing the joint— it was among the three taverns (Melby's over on Aurora was another) involved in the scandalous case of a WSLCB inspector who was charged with seeking cash bribes "on an understanding that he would protect the tavern owner in each case against official action for alleged sales of beer to minors.…The tavern operators named in the charges said they had sold no beer or wine to minors, but paid anyway to avoid trouble."

By the early 1950s, the Inn was being managed by Wes Moore, who was known for having installed a mechanical music box inside of his wooden leg—one that surprised patrons by playing the old ditty "How Dry I Am." Meanwhile, in 1958, Haines patented his musical spoons instrument, which he, performing as Mr. Spoons, showed off on ABC-TV's popular *Lawrence Welk Show*. In the wake of that exposure, spooning became a nationwide fad that brought Haines considerable commercial success.

Top: Fiddler's Inn matchbook, undated. *Courtesy Northwest Music Archives.*

Bottom: Fiddler's Inn, 1941. *Courtesy Puget Sound Regional Archives.*

Years flew by, then around Thanksgiving Day in 1992, Fiddler's Inn made the news when a prankster friend promised the then-current owner, Frank Genta, the gift of a "fresh" turkey—only for Genta to soon discover a live eighteen-pounder let loose inside the building. Genta phoned the Progressive Animal Welfare Society (PAWS) to donate the big bird, and their rep quipped: "We've always argued that animals don't belong behind bars. They don't belong in bars, either. *Wild Turkey*, maybe—but a tame turkey, never." In 1995, new owners bought the Inn, remodeled it and have continued the tradition of pouring beer for thirsty guests ever since. The Fiddler's Inn also specializes in pizza, and many a musician has gigged here in modern times, including Heather Banker & Jack Cook, Blue Madness, Bobcat Bob & Frisco Charlie, Jimmy Free, Don Goodwin Jazz Trio, Harmonia Pocket, Michael Iris, Scott Law, Scandia Kapell, Kimball & the Fugitives, Muddy & the Wigerians, Pekka Penlik, Rai, Chris Skyhawk and Toad Jam.

Mack's Shanty

This survivor is perhaps *the* classic case of a roadhouse being situated in an actual house along a road. It was originally built in 1932 on Twenty-Second Avenue Northeast, and in 1937, Doris V. McLoed recast the place as a "beer parlor," Mack's Shanty. In time it was moved a bit to 8816 Bothell Way, just south of the old Willard's Inn site. Later—under the ownership of Doris's son Bill "Mack" McLoed—it began featuring live music at night. By 1941, it had moved to a location several lots northward (to 8904 and then to 8916 Bothell Way), then it moved again around 1948 to 9002 Bothell Way, where it boasted a sizable parking lot in which local hot rod clubs were fond of rallying. The year 1961 saw the business sold to John Spaccarotelli, who shortened its name to the Shanty, and it continued as a popular dive where folks could drink, play pool and darts and dance to live music.

A few early '60s Seattle rock bands, including the Accents, gigged here, and in more recent times many others followed, including Blacktop Deceiver, Doll Squad, DTs, Billy Dwayne and the Creepers, Fabulous Hammers, F-Holes, Glad Girls, Groggy Bikini, Industry People, Jaguar Paw, Johnny7 & the Black Crabs, Los Peligrosos, Lost Dogma, Mama Tried, Moonspinners,

Mack's Shanty, shown receiving a shipment of beer kegs by the Sunset Bottling Co. distributorship, 1941. *Courtesy Puget Sound Regional Archives.*

The Mrs. Bill Larsens, NW Rivals, 1234, Petunia, Riffbrokers, Shaken Growlers, Speed Mop, Thee Sargent Major 3 and the Vipers. For several years, the Shanty hosted KCMU DJ Leon Berman's *Shake the Shack Rockabilly Ball* car show, and meanwhile, various modern country bands also gigged here, including Country Dave, Country Lips, Ruby Dee and the Snake Handlers, Lavender Country, Pete Marshall & the New Broke West, Christy McWilson, 1 Uppers, Rainieros and the Western Bluebirds. Along the way, the Shanty has been proudly promoted as "the last roadhouse in Seattle."

BIBLIOGRAPHY

Archival Materials

National Archives at Seattle. McNeil Island Penitentiary Prisoner Identification Photographs 1875–ca. 1923, United States Penitentiary, Record of Prisoners Received, Harold Ira Parker, Register No. 13347, ARC: 608846; Bureau of Prisons, Record Number 129.

Seattlife. "The Late Hotel Butler." April 1939. Accessed via Vic Meyers clipping file at the Seattle Public Library.

Sherwood, Don. "Burke-Gilman Trail," in "Interpretive Essays of the Histories of Seattle's Parks and Playfields." Handwritten bound manuscript. N.p., 1977. Seattle Room, Seattle Public Library.

Willard's. "Not a Roadhouse" graphic ad, Orpheum Circuit News and Program, Seattle, February 1924, p. 5–6.

Books and Miscellaneous Publications

Blecha, Peter. *Music in Washington: Seattle and Beyond.* Charleston, SC: Arcadia Publishing, 2007.

Broderick, Henry. *Early Seattle Profiles.* Seattle, WA: Dogwood Press, 1959.

Caster, Dick. *The Brooklake Community Center.* Federal Way, WA: Historical Society of Federal Way, 2017.

de Barros, Paul. *Jackson Street After Hours: The Roots of Jazz in Seattle.* Seattle, WA: Sasquatch Books, 1993.

Flood, Chuck. *Washington's Highway 99.* Charleston, SC: Arcadia Publishing, 2013.

Holden, Brad. *Seattle Prohibition: Bootleggers, Rumrunners and Graft in the Queen City.* Charleston, SC: The History Press, 2019.

Jones, Quincy. *Q: The Autobiography of Quincy Jones.* New York: Harlem Moon/Broadway Books, 2002.

Little, Marie, Kevin K. Stadler and the Alderwood Manor Heritage Association. *Alderwood Manor.* Charleston, SC: Arcadia Publishing, 2006.

Marsh, Dave. *Louie Louie: The History and Mythology of the World's Most Famous Rock 'n' Roll Song […].* New York: Hyperion, 1993.

McDonald, Wally. "A 49 Year Musical History of the Northwest." Unpublished memoir, pdf in author's possession.

Nordheim, Teresa. *Wicked Seattle.* Charleston, SC: The History Press, 2020.

Wegener, Otto Frederick. *The Crämer Case: A Drama from German-American Life–How To Fabricate Evidence Against a Helpless German Worker—Authentic Representation of the Famous Criminal Case.* Tacoma, WA: Druck Der "Wacht Am Sunde," 1896.

Whitcomb, Ian. *Rock Odyssey.* New York: Doubleday/Dolphin, 1983.

Interviews

Coryell, Larry. Interview with Peter Blecha. 1984.

Gaeng, Betty Lou. Interviews with Brad Holden. 2020–21.

Hendrix, Al. Interviews with Peter Blecha. 1978–94.

Spaccarotelli, Dayna. Emails to Peter Blecha. November 2021–January 2022.

Newspapers

Articles are cited first by name of author or newspaper, then by date of publication.

Badcon, Marian. "The Lakes on the Crest." *Seattle Post-Intelligencer*, September 28, 1924.

Bermann, R.B. "Bacchus Was Butler Prohisaver." *Seattle Post-Intelligencer*, March 15, 1929.

Case, Frederick. "How Dry It Wasn't." *Pacific*, October 30, 1983.

Cleary, Caitlin, Paul de Barros, and Melanie McFarland. "Controversy Has Dogged Music for Decades." *Seattle Times*, October 1, 2000. https://archive.seattletimes.com/archive/?date=20001001&slug=4045501.

Cunningham, Ross. "When Rose Room Was the Place." *Seattle Times*, July 15, 1977.

Edmonds Tribune-Review. "Deputies Raid Road House on Highway." November 26, 1926.

———. "Road Houses Raided." January 6, 1928.

———. "More Arrests Made at 'Doc' Hamilton's." March 16, 1928.

———. "Road House Is in Ruins." March 8, 1929.

———. "Inn Operator Battles Bandit." April 11, 1930.

———. "Blakewood Inn Destroyed by Fire Monday." March 24, 1935.

Everett Daily Herald. "Safecrackers Fail in Ranch Attempt." September 28, 1939.

———. "Spectacular Fire Destroys El Rancho Sunday Morning." May 28, 1959.

Niendorff, Fred. "Bannick Nets 4 in Tour of Roadhouses," *Seattle Post-Intelligencer*, February 7, 1927.

Northwest Enterprise. "Citizens Protest against 'Coon' Chicken Inn." September 18, 1930.

Reddin, John J. "Seattle's Gastronomic, Economic History Reflected by Eating Houses through Years," *Seattle Times*, August 21, 1960.

Seattle Daily Intelligencer. "A Big Blaze." May 8, 1878.

———. "Made Room." May 9, 1878.

Seattle Times. "Hodge Takes His Tip from Times and Raids Duffy's Roadhouse." November 4, 1911.

———. "Hodge Sleeps While Roadhouses on Golf Club Road Run Wide." December 22, 1911.

———. "New Road Planned." October 20, 1919.

———. "Humes Expedites Paving Projects." February 22, 1920.

———. "Booze Blamed for Killing! Prosecutor Says Lacelle Slaying Calls for Action." October 8, 1923.

———. "Night Owl Visits Roadhouses Seeks Jazz and Refreshments." October 12, 1923.

———. "4 Arrested by Sheriff in Round of Taverns." December 26, 1923.

———. "Inn Owner Arrested." June 1, 1924.

———. "Three Men Escape Death in Accident on Highway." November 3, 1924.

———. "Unique Place of Entertainment." Rotogravure Pictorial Section, March 15, 1925.

———. "Announcing the Opening of the Jungle Temple." July 20, 1925.

———. "Rum Doesn't Worry Juror." January 20, 1926.

———. "Bush & Lane Piano Co. Announce the Installation of Magnola… at Willard's." Display ad, March 8, 1927.

———. "Three Escape Death as Car Overturns." March 16, 1927.

———. "'Doc' Hamilton Waits in Jail, Denies He Knew of Gambling." April 4, 1927.

———. "Butler Hotel Rum Raid Nets 17 Men, Women." November 14, 1927.

———. "Officers Seize Ancient Roulette Wheel and Bottled Goods at Snohomish Taverns." January 2, 1928.

———. "Dry Office Will Seek Abatement of Roadhouses." January 3, 1928.

———. "Road Houses Raided." January 6, 1928.

———. "Judgment Obtained on Barbecue Ranch." January 31, 1928.

———. "Woman Posts Bail after Night in Jail." February 19, 1928.

———. "More Arrests Made at 'Doc' Hamilton's." March 16, 1928.

———. "U.S. Seeks Abatement of 'Doc' Hamilton's Place." April 6, 1928.

———. "Meat Market Owner Is Sued for Divorce." May 16, 1928.

———. "Dance Hall Noisy, Close It, Residents Ask Board." September 11, 1928.

———. "Roadhouse Raid Yields List of Many Patrons." September 24, 1928.

———. "Burning of M'Kenzie Roadhouse Mystifies—Racketeering May Have Caused Second Blaze." March 5, 1929.

———. "Road House Is in Ruins." March 8, 1929.

———. "Closing of Rose Room at 9 p.m. Expected." March 24, 1929.

———. "2 Employes in Hamilton Booze Trial Are Guilty." June 27, 1929.

———. "Hits by Mrs.—The Lady Has This to Say." June 30, 1929.

———. "Liquor Abatement Is Filed against Hamilton Barbecue." August 14, 1929.

———. "Five Men Arrested When Dry Squad Raids Roadhouse." October 21, 1929.

———. "Dry Agents to Tell about Night Life." November 17, 1929.

———. "Inn Operator Battles Bandit." April 11, 1930.

———. "Rose Room to Open Tonight as Ban Lifts." May 7, 1930.

———. "Inn Under Guard after Bomb Threat." September 21, 1930.

———. "Dinner to Brown Nearly Disrupted by Rum Search." January 11, 1931.

———. "Bothell Highway Inns Open—Chicken Dinner Time Arrives on Famous Drive." May 22, 1931.

———. "'Old Man River' Flows Deep Blue for Doc Hamilton." May 26, 1931.

———. "Auto and Liquor Seized; Pair Jailed." October 21, 1931.

———. "New Dry Head Opens War on 'Flask Toters.'" December 7, 1931.

———. "Children Frolic, Rum Flows, Say Resort Reports." January 12, 1932.

———. "Blakehart Inn's License Revoked by Commissioners." January 18, 1932.

———. "Bannock to Aid U.S. Dries in Padlocking." January 26, 1932.

———. "Doc Hamilton Resort Abated by Cushman." June 8, 1932.

———. "Dreher Divots." March 2, 1933.

———. "After Flames Danced." July 5, 1933.

———. "Favors and Fun Promised Club Cotton Patrons." February 21, 1934.

———. "Blakewood Inn Destroyed by Fire Monday." March 24, 1935.

———. "4 Beer Parlors Lose Licenses." May 28, 1935.

———. "Woman Asks for $25,000 for Fall at Roadhouse." June 5, 1935.

———. "Four Arrested in Roadhouse Raid." July 15, 1935.

———. "State Officers Raid 'The Ranch.'" January 24, 1936.

———. "The Charmland, New Highway Spot, Opens Tonight." August 16, 1936.

———. "'Doc' Hamilton Denies Liquor; Pays $50 Fine." October 3, 1936.

———. "Club Charmland Opens Tomorrow with New Show." December 18, 1936.

———. "Grand Opening Saturday Night Club Charmland." December 18, 1936.

———. "At the Bagdad—Meet Doc Hamilton." January 3, 1937.

———. "'Doc' Hamilton, Club Operator, Is Dead at 51." September 8, 1942.

———. "15 Arrested in Raid on Roadhouse." August 6, 1944.

———. "Former Deputy, Assistant Fined on Gambling Charge." October 5, 1944.

———. "Raiding of Tipped-Off Gambling Den Is Like the Movies—Only Funnier." September 10, 1945.

———. "Lew Still Free, Sheriff Rapped." September 17, 1945.

———. "Sale to Minors Suspends Bar." October 8, 1945.

———. "Lew Found Guilty as Gambler." January 13, 1946.

————. "City Approves License for New Cabaret." February 19, 1946.

————. "Eight Rural Restaurants Seek Cocktail Lounges." March 22, 1949.

————. "Grand Re-Opening—El Rancho." January 24, 1952.

————. "Music-Lovers Eye That Wooden Leg." November 23, 1952.

————. "Gambling Runs Openly in Night Club Near Lynnwood," April 16, 1956.

————. "20 Arrested in Snohomish County Bookmaking Raid." April 22, 1956.

————. "Minors Seen Drinking in Roadhouse." December 3, 1956.

————. "El Rancho Owner Has No Plans to Rebuild Burned Roadhouse." May 25, 1959.

————. "Spectacular Fire Destroys El Rancho Sunday Morning." May 28, 1959.

————. "Old China Pheasant Destroyed." September 2, 1965.

————. "Faces of the City." October 26, 1966.

Seattle Post Intelligencer. "County Has Big Highway Plan." February 1, 1920.

————. "Would Call Route Victory Way." March 7, 1920.

————. "Roadhouse Staff Held over Booze." December 1, 1923.

————. "Florist Accused of Transporting Liquor." July 1, 1924.

————. "Traffic Jams Victory Way." July 28, 1924.

————. "Five Men Are Held in Moonshine Raid." September 9, 1924.

————. "Bannick Attacks Roadhouse Evil." August 27, 1926.

————. "This Camel Hysterical after Raid." January 2, 1927.

————. "U.S. Drys Raid 2 Roadhouses." January 9, 1927.

————. "Roadhouse Guests Face Rum Arrest." March 1, 1927.

————. "Drys Mop Up Road Houses." April 4, 1927.

————. "Two Jointists Plead Guilty." May 14, 1927.

————. "Run Raid Ends in Free Fight." July 18, 1927.

————. "'Doc' Hamilton Crosses Line." August 6, 1927.

————. "Court Rough on Roadhouses." December 15, 1927.

————. "Prosecutor Is Backed by Volstead Act." December 24, 1927.

————. "Three Alleged Joints Closed." December 25, 1927.

————. "Doc Hamilton Faces Sheriff." January 1, 1928.

————. "15 Arrested as Drys Mop Roadhouses." January 2, 1928.

————. "Roadhouses Face Padlock over Liquor." January 3, 1928.

————. "Melby Is Held in Liquor Raid Quiz." March 1, 1928.

————. "Doc Hamilton's Barbecue May Be Padlocked." April 6, 1928.

————. "Seattle Folk Caught among Tavern Guests." June 17, 1929.

————. "Wife of Dance Hall Head Wins Divorce." August 10, 1929.

———. "Five Arrested by Dry Raider at the Ranch." October 21, 1929.

———. "Jungle Temple Raided Again." December 17, 1929.

———. "Graft War Told Hartley by 'Secret 10.'" November 20, 1931.

———. "Padlock Asked for the Ranch." January 16, 1932.

———. "Society Liquor Dealer Guilty." March 13, 1932.

———. "Neterer Sentences Florist-Bootlegger." March 22, 1932.

———. "Jolly Roger in Debut on Bothell Way." June 29, 1934.

———. "Jolly Roger, New Roadhouse, to Offer Patrons Three-fold Service." June 29, 1934.

———. "Three New Dine and Dance Establishments Announce Opening Dates." June 29, 1934.

———. "State Police Invade Two Roadhouses." July 1, 1935.

———. "Licenses of Three Taverns Canceled by State Control Board." August 13, 1935.

———. "State Liquor Men 'Store' Clubs Bar." December 12, 1936.

———. "Grand Jury Gets Still Seizure Case." December 19, 1936.

———. "Dance Place's Plan Gala Fares." December 20, 1935.

———. "Formal Opening Tonight the Jolly Roger." December 20, 1935.

———. "Big Tree Inn Moves to a New Location." August 9, 1938.

———. "China Pheasant Opening Tonight." August 27, 1940.

———. "War Stymies Business Men of Roadsides." November 29, 1942.

———. "On the Home Front." December 6, 1942.

———. "Carl Melby Dies." December 8, 1942.

———. "Harry Lew Gets 5 Years on Charge." February 20, 1946.

———. "El Rancho to Open." March 23, 1946.

———. "Lew Released from Prison." August 19, 1947.

———. "Liquor Bribe Charges Filed." August 28, 1949.

———. "Equipment Taken in Raid on Pheasant." April 2, 1955.

———. "After Hours Drinking Place Again Raided." April 16, 1962.

———. "Old China Pheasant Destroyed." September 2, 1965.

———. "Fire Razes Old China Restaurant." September 3, 1965.

———. "Turkey's Delight." November 25, 1992.

Skreen, Chet. "Seattle-Tacoma's Big-Ballroom Days." *Seattle Times*, November 9, 1975.

Suffia, David. "The Saga of 'Doc' Hamilton." *Seattle Times*, April 1, 1974.

Watts, Alice. "When the Big Bands and the Big Names Played Olympia," *Totem*, November 13, 1983.

Online Articles

Becker, Paula. "Governor Clarence Martin Signs the Steele Act Establishing the Washington State Liquor Control Board on January 23, 1934." HistoryLink.org, January 17, 2011. https://www.historylink.org/File/9692.

Berger, Knute. "Auto Reverie: The Daze of Seattle's First Cars." Crosscut, October 8, 2013. https://crosscut.com/2013/10/seattle-cars-autos.

Blecha, Peter. "Evergreen Ballroom." HistoryLink.org, March 14, 2011. https://www.historylink.org/File/9557.

———. "Parker's Ballroom." HistoryLink.org, June 5, 2002. https://www.historylink.org/File/3827.

———. "Spanish Castle Ballroom." HistoryLink.org, May 24, 2002. https://www.historylink.org/File/3826.

Bunn, Valarie. "Gerhard Ericksen's Good Road." *Wedgwood in Seattle History* (blog), August 26, 2013. https://wedgwoodinseattlehistory.com/2013/08/26/gerhard-ericksens-good-road/.

———. "Walter Haines, Founder of the Fiddler's Inn, Wedgwood." *Wedgwood in Seattle History* (blog), September 10, 2012. https://wedgwoodinseattlehistory.com/2012/09/10/walter-haines-founder-of-the-fiddlers-inn-wedgwood/.

Covert, Nancy. "Bresemann, E. J. (1881–1971)." HistoryLink.org, September 18, 2009. https://www.historylink.org/File/9156.

Dawson, Raechel. "Book Tells Brooklake Community Center's Storied Past." *Federal Way Mirror*, March 27, 2017. https://www.federalwaymirror.com/life/book-tells-brooklake-community-centers-storied-past/.

Dougherty, Phil. "Seattle-Everett Highway Opens on October 26, 1927." HistoryLink.org, April 22, 2020.

Gaeng, Betty Lou. "Looking Back: The Birth and Evolution of Highway 99 in South Snohomish County." *My Edmonds News*, May 26, 2018. https://myedmondsnews.com/2018/05/looking-back-the-birth-and-evolution-of-highway-99-in-south-snohomish-county/.

———. "Looking Back: The Birth and Evolution of Highway 99 in South Snohomish County, Part 2." *My Edmonds News*, May 27, 2018. https://myedmondsnews.com/2018/05/looking-back-the-birth-and-evolution-of-highway-99-in-south-snohomish-county-part-2/.

Holden, Brad. "Prohibition in the Puget Sound Region 1916–1933." HistoryLink.org, November 18, 2019. https://www.historylink.org/File/20904.

Long, Priscilla. "Madame Lou Graham Arrives in Seattle in February 1888." HistoryLink.org, January 1, 2000. https://www.historylink.org/File/2762.

Michelson, Alan. "Illahee, Pioneer Square, Seattle, WA." Pacific Coast Architecture Database. http://pcad.lib.washington.edu/building/20008/.

Roth, Catherine. "Coon Chicken Inn Seattle." HistoryLink.org, October 16, 2009. https://www.historylink.org/File/9191.

Shoreline Area News (blog). "Parker's Casino and Sports Bar May Be Headed for Demolition." August 21, 2012. https://www.shorelineareanews.com/2012/08/parkers-casino-and-sports-bar-may-be.html.

Shoreline Historical Museum. "Where Have All the Dance Halls Gone?" Facebook posting, February 10, 2017.

Stiles, Vicki. "Roadhouses, Restaurants and Refreshments—The Jolly Roger and the Coon Chicken Inn." seattlepi.com, April 4, 2007. https://blog.seattlepi.com/lakecity/2007/04/04/blast-from-the-past-12/.

Vogel, Larry. "Transforming Highway 99: Roadway Has Roots as Major Highway—and a Hotbed of Vice." *My Edmonds News*, May 11, 2018. https://myedmondsnews.com/2018/05/transforming-highway-99-roadway-has-roots-as-major-highway-and-a-hotbed-of-vice/.

Washington's Pacific Highway. "The Historic Pacific Highway in Washington." http://www.pacific-hwy.net/.

Special thanks to Leslie Ann Meyer, MLIS, genealogy research consultant.

ABOUT THE AUTHORS

Peter Blecha is a staff historian with HistoryLink.org, the director of the Northwest Music Archives and an award-winning author of nine books. A longtime member of the Pacific Northwest Historians Guild and former longtime senior curator at Seattle's EMP music museum (today's MoPop), Blecha has been acknowledged over the decades as "the premier expert in his chosen field of research" (*Seattle Weekly*, 1988), "Seattle's best-known collector" (*Scram Magazine*, 2006), the "Indiana Jones of Rock 'n' Roll" (The *Rocket*, 2000) and a writer who "deserves a place in Northwest music history for his important role in preserving its history and promoting its legacy" (*Seattle Post-Intelligencer*, 2005).

Brad Holden writes a monthly column for *Seattle Magazine*, is a contributing writer for HistoryLink.org and is one of the hosts of the popular podcast *Dim Lights & Stiff Drinks: The Dive Bars of Seattle*. His work has also appeared in *Pacific Northwest Magazine*. Holden has been profiled by *Seattle Refined*, KUOW, *King 5 Evening!* and *Art Zone with Nancy Guppy*, as well as various newspapers. His first book, *Seattle Prohibition: Bootleggers, Rumrunners and Graft in the Queen City*, was published in 2019 and made several recommended reading lists, including the Seattle Public Library's "Best Books of 2019" and *Seattle Metropolitan Magazine*'s "Big Seattle Reading List." *Lost Roadhouses of Seattle* is his third book.